Johan Grimonprez

Looking for Alfred

STUART
CROFT
FOUNDATION

'Who says there's only two of us,' he said mischievously, 'maybe there's three…
or four of us.'

Hitchcock double in *Double Take*, Johan Grimonprez

I'VE DECIDED N

SOME ONE ELSE

~~By an odd coinc~~

~~have a story ab~~

~~decided to be so~~

~~than himself,~~ In

coincidence that man Appears

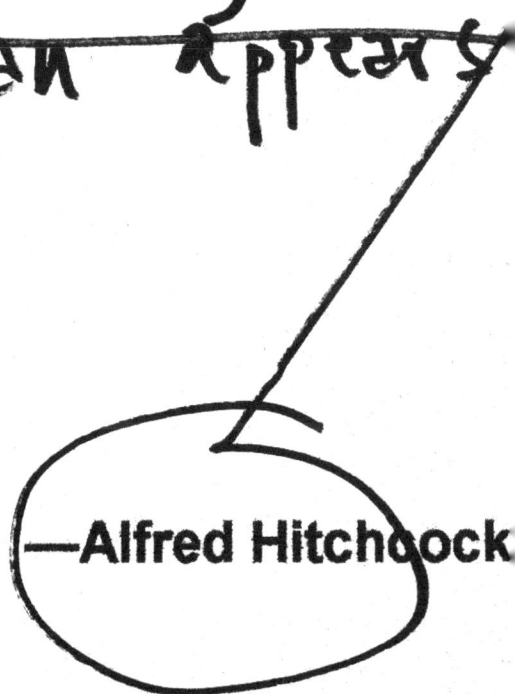

—Alfred Hitchcock

begin of book

TO BE AFTER ALL ...

~~dence we~~

~~ut a man who~~

~~meone other~~

~~by an equally odd~~

~~o look like me~~

Alfred HITCHCOCK in: NONE ARE SO BLIND.

Alfred Hitchcock Presents: "None are so blind"

The Hitchcock Castings

Johan Grimonprez

Looking for Alfred

Texts by
Patricia Allmer
Jorge Luis Borges
Chris Darke
Thomas Elsaesser
Tom McCarthy
Jeff Noon
Slavoj Žižek

Edited by
Steven Bode

Photography by
Theo Volpatti
Mathias Kessler
Daragh Reeves
Kristien Daem

Contents

Who is this man? Who is the real Alfred Hitchcock? I shall begin by correcting several misconceptions about myself, which have grown up over the years. It is high time I set the record straight…

I am certain that you are wondering how such a story got started. It began nearly 40 years ago. As you know, I make a brief appearance in each of my pictures. One of the earliest of these was *The Lodger*, the story of Jack the Ripper. My appearance called for me to walk up the stairs of the rooming house. Since my walk-ons in subsequent pictures would be equally strenuous… casting – with an unusual lack of perception – hired this fat man! The rest is history. He became the public image of Hitchcock. Changing the image was impossible. Therefore I had to conform to the image. It was not easy. But proof of my success is that no one has ever noticed the difference.

Our cherubic friend had a tragic ending. It was during the 1940s while he was trying desperately to make an appearance in a picture. Unfortunately Tallulah Bankhead wouldn't allow him to climb into the lifeboat. She was afraid he'd sink it. It was rather sad watching him go down. Of course, we could have saved him, but it would have meant ruining the take…

You may be sure that in securing an actor for my next picture I was more careful. I gave casting an accurate and detailed description of my true self. Casting did an expert job. The result: Cary Grant in *Notorious*.

As you know, I still remain a prisoner of the old image. They say that inside every fat man is a thin man trying desperately to get out. Now you know that the thin man is the real Alfred Hitchcock.

Alfred Hitchcock's after-dinner speech at the Screen Producers' Guild Dinner, March 7, 1965 in 'Hitchcock on Hitchcock: Selected Writings and Interviews' by Edward Allardice, ed. Sidney Gottlieb; University of California Press, Berkeley and Los Angeles, 1995.

**The length of a film should be
directly related to the endurance
of the human bladder.**

Alfred Hitchcock

Sometir
is just a

Sigmund Freud

es a cigar

cigar.

Foreword

Ten years ago, in 1997, the Belgian artist Johan Grimonprez stepped forward into the spotlight of international attention. The scene of this event was in Germany, at documenta X in Kassel, and the occasion was the premiere of *Dial H-I-S-T-O-R-Y*, a complex film collage combining the history of skyjackings with the history of media that drew from multiple image sources, sampling news footage, documentary, and commercial advertising. Both provocative and playful, *Dial H-I-S-T-O-R-Y* revealed in a very distinctive and original way that truth and falsehood, reality and fiction must be seen as fluid, overlapping and easily manipulable dimensions.

Johan Grimonprez is a slow worker and a fast one at the same time. A quick-witted thinker constantly chasing and juggling ideas, Grimonprez also works extremely slowly, burrowing deeper and deeper into his projects, which as a consequence take on proportions, and arrive at destinations, that nobody could have fully foreseen at the start. What can be predicted with certainty, however, is that a work by Johan Grimonprez will be likely to span a number of years.

So it is with *Looking for Alfred*. Begun in 2003, this project has led the artist on a pursuit which can sometimes appear to be never-ending. In the intervening years, Grimonprez has produced a video installation, and a short film for cinemas, a video of the casting sessions undertaken for the film, and, on top of that, hundreds of original hand drawings, collages and photographs that accompany the working process. *Looking for Alfred* premiered in London and Brussels in 2004, has received numerous international stagings and several prestigious awards, while Grimonprez's current feature-length film project, *Double Take*, extends and develops many of its themes.

With *Looking for Alfred* as its centrepiece, Pinakothek der Moderne in Munich is delighted to present a mid-career survey of Johan Grimonprez's work – ten years after his first appearance to a broader art public. On the event of his first solo exhibition at a major museum in Germany, Pinakothek and Film and Video Umbrella are equally pleased to collaborate on a large-scale publication, which like the exhibition itself, highlights not only Grimonprez's work with moving images, but also his drawings, which represent such a significant focus of the exhibition as realised in Munich.

We would like to express our sincere thanks to everyone involved in the exhibition and this publication.

Reinhold Baumstark, General Director, Bayerische Staatsgemäldesammlungen, Pinakothek der Moderne
Steven Bode, Director, Film and Video Umbrella

You'd see people in the street
do double-takes, whispering:
'Oh, that man looks like
Hitchcock!', 'Look, look!
It's Alfred!'

I was slimmer then, you know.
But I didn't know at the time
I actually resembled Hitchcock;
when you look in the mirror,
you can never see yourself the
way others see you.

Ron Burrage, Hitchcock double

Two goats in a junkyard chew on a reel of film. One goat says to the other: 'I liked the book better.'

Cartoon in Hitchcock's office

Introduction

A book of a film, or a film of a book, is never quite the same as the original. Despite the fact that they often share the same name, the two things are cut from very different cloth – no matter how closely they follow the same story, or faithfully render its constituent scenes, they will never be totally identical; a part and yet apart. Like the work of art and its mechanical reproduction, the one is a mirror image of the other; which, for all its tantalising likeness, leads a separate, and vicarious, existence. A double of its subject, a representation that is also always a translation, it not only extends its presence in the world, but slowly and ineluctably starts to change it from what it once was.

These thoughts seem particularly apposite in the case of the Belgian artist, Johan Grimonprez. In a series of (mostly) film and video works dating from the early Nineties, and including the coruscating *Dial H-I-S-T-O-R-Y* (1997), Grimonprez looks at contemporary society through a glass darkly, magnifying its tics and obsessions, and bringing its underlying dreams and fears into sharper, starker focus. Although his pieces are frequently distinguished by their energy and offbeat humour, there are sophisticated insights also into the complex mechanics of a media spectacle that all-too-quickly turns real events into pseudo-events, and where History is increasingly played back to us as second-hand copycat culture. His images themselves, including many plundered from archive sources, do their own little bit, of course, to explode the fast-diminishing boundaries that used to separate the original from the copy, and while highlighting his flair for a telling and startling juxtaposition, often force us to a do a double-take, to look again at what we first thought to be true. Nowhere more so, perhaps, than in his latest work *Looking for Alfred* (2004), a virtuoso study of the phenomenon of the lookalike that takes his longstanding fascination with identity and celebrity, with selfhood, simulation and commodity, to extraordinary new heights.

Looking for Alfred is such a gargantuan and audacious undertaking that even a book twice the size of this already substantial volume would be hard pressed to cover all its various facets and phases. Originally conceived as an elaborate *hommage* to the films of Alfred Hitchcock, as seen through the prism of the director's many cameo appearances in his own movies, it has grown to incorporate an ever-increasing number of other walk-on parts, mostly by the diverse bunch of Hitchcock doubles that Grimonprez auditioned for roles in his eventual film. Carried out in New York, Los Angeles, Gent, Rotterdam and London, these 'screen tests' have also been assiduously documented in countless photographs and untold hours of videotape, and, like the equally detailed storyboards and drawings by Grimonprez that chart the genesis and development of the project, form an absolutely integral part of the work – as pivotal to it as the projected loop that is the ostensible centerpiece of its public manifestations, where it has been shown in both a cinema setting and as a gallery-based installation.

Indeed, rather than the casting material being thought of as a disposable, transitional prelude to the finished film, it is more accurate, perhaps, to think of the film as a kind of trailer for a much wider project, in which the film / loop / trailer (call it what you will), and so much that was essential to the process of making it, are showcased side by side. Since *Looking for Alfred* has had a habit of morphing and mutating over the course of its four-year history, it would be premature to consider even this, or any other, expanded version of the project as the absolute finished article. With this in mind, it is interesting to observe that a new and different side of *Looking for Alfred* is already starting to emerge, tracing the story of one of its key protagonists, Ron Burrage, and his own successful double life as a professional Hitchcock impersonator. Giving further screen-time to Hitchcock's penchant for playing with his own identity (and not only in his regular cameo roles), it contrasts Hitchcock the Movie Maestro with his popular televisual alter ego as the deliciously droll master of ceremonies in his long-running TV series *Alfred Hitchcock Presents*; a shift in persona that is employed by Grimonprez as part of a wider face-off between cinema and its upstart mini-me, television.

Published on the occasion of a major exhibition at Pinakothek der Moderne in Munich, this book is both a unique visual record of the evolution of *Looking for Alfred* and a discrete and parallel chapter of it. Extending many of its recurring themes into a more obviously literary areas, and enlisting authors, with a predilection for doubles, such as Jorge Luis Borges, Edgar Allan Poe and Jeff Noon, the publication foregrounds the ideas and interests that have done so much to inform the direction of the work. Although Hitchcock looms as large as ever across its pages, there is a comparable space carved out for the formative influence of the artist René Magritte, whose acute reflections on the nuances of perception and the vicissitudes of representation add a further conceptual resonance, and whose iconic paintings, such as *La Reproduction interdite* and *Jeune fille mangeant un oiseau (Le Plaisir)*, hover, with the force of archetypes, behind Grimonprez's cinematic tableaux. Last but not least, amongst all these multiple voices, the book offers a platform for Grimonprez himself, in an extended in-conversation section, to expand upon his underlying intentions and preoccupations.

A publication of this scale only ever comes about through the input of a number of different partners. Film and Video Umbrella is proud to have been involved with *Looking for Alfred* almost from the outset, and is equally pleased to be working in such close collaboration with Pinakothek der Moderne on a book which both organisations are confident will be a fitting testament to such a powerful and memorable work. Our colleagues at our respective institutions have given us invaluable assistance throughout and we would like to single out in particular Nina Ernst and Caroline Smith (from Film and Video Umbrella) and Carla Schulz-Hoffmann (from Pinakothek), as well as Michael Van Peel and Emmy Oost (from Zapomatik). Pinakothek is especially grateful to the Theo Wormland Stiftung, and its chairman Hartwig Garnerus, whose support of both the exhibition and the publication has been crucial in helping us realise the extent of our ambitions.

The partnership on the publication does not end there. *Looking for Alfred* would not be the piece it is without the generous initial support of the Centre for Fine Arts in Brussels (where a large part of the production took place, and whose distinctive interiors figure prominently in the film). After receiving its Belgian avant-premiere there in December 2004, *Looking for Alfred* then formed a major component of a further exhibition, 'Revolution/Restoration' (curated by Dirk Snauwaert and Barbara Vanderlinden). As a re-affirmation of this crucial early interest, their additional investment in the book is one for which we are particularly grateful. Our thanks go the Centre's Director, Paul Dujardin, and also to Sophie Lauwers, exhibition co-ordinator. We also acknowledge a generous contribution from SMAK, Museum of Contemporary Art, Gent, who have given additional support to the publication and who will host the Pinakothek der Moderne exhibition in Belgium in the near future. For the assistance they have given to the publication and the production, we acknowledge the input of Sean Kelly, Jeffrey Deitch and Hisami Kuroiwa, and for the key support they have given to the many aspects of this project, we would like to thank the Flemish Authorities and Arts Council England.

We would also like to thank Hatje Cantz for adding their own considerable weight to the publication, which has enhanced its ambitions in numerous different ways. For their highly original and provocative texts, we should save a special mention for the writers Tom McCarthy, Thomas Elsaesser, Patricia Allmer and Chris Darke. We are grateful also to Slavoj Žižek and Jeff Noon for allowing us to reprint their two texts, and to Maria Kodama for her kind permission to include the story 'August 25, 1983' by Jorge Luis Borges.

For his distinctive and unifying design work, whose visual flair belies its sizeable logistical complexity, we owe a particular debt of gratitude to Herman Lelie, and to Stefania Bonelli. Finally, though, our thanks go to Johan Grimonprez, whose contribution to this publication, as an individual and as part of the production team at Zapomatik, has been immense. We have greatly enjoyed our journey together on this project.

Steven Bode, Director, Film and Video Umbrella
Bernhart Schwenk, Chief Curator, Pinakothek der Moderne

® hitch meets hitch:

19

→

'STAGE FRIGHT' (1950)

+

REIGN ORRESPONDENT' (1940)

↓

Alfred Hitchcock Lookalikes Casting

Reply to: see below
Date: 2004-04-14, 11:21AM PDT

"Looking For Alfred", Johan Grimonprez director.
If you resemble Alfred Hitchcock, please send or deliver a
picture to:
Emily Schweber, Casting Director
5225 Wilshire Blvd. Suite 718
L.A. CA 90036

Deadline April 19
Film to shoot in June in London.
Casting open to any age (over 18), and any ethnicity.

Compensation: Scale pay plus all travel and expenses
Principals only. Recruiters, please don't contact this job poster.
Please, no phone calls about this job!
Please do not contact job poster about other services, products
or commercial interests.
Reposting this message elsewhere is OK.
this is in or around Los Angeles

Casting

00:23:30:15   Z50

                       MF55

┌   ┐

                       F8.0

└   ┘

              38min

PowerBook G4

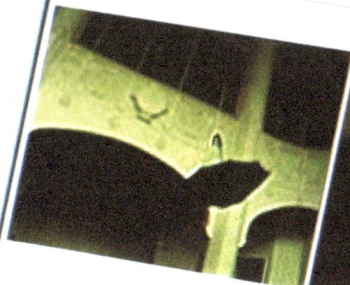
002ab_P7254953.JPG

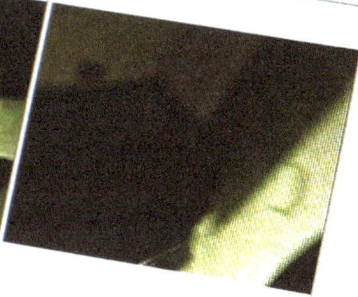
003ab_004ab_P7234255...

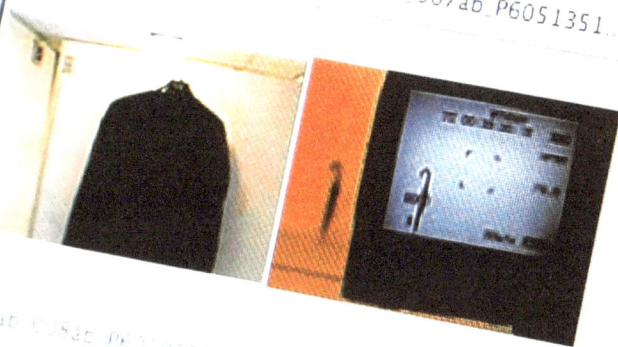

005ab_006ab_P6051349

006ab_007ab_P6051351...

007ab_008ab_P6010639

008ab_010ab_P6010286...

009ab_DSC01162.JPG

010ab_011ab_with his o...

98 item(s)

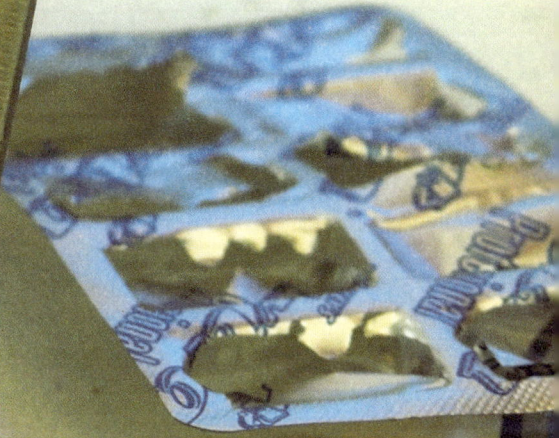

It might be a Scottish name, taken from a story about two men in a train. One man says, 'What's that package up there in the luggage rack?'

And the other answers, 'Oh, that's a MacGuffin.'

The first one asks, 'What's a MacGuffin?'

'Well,' the other man says, 'It's an apparatus for trapping lions in the Scottish Highlands.' Then the first man says 'But there are no lions in the Scottish Highlands,' and the other answers 'Well then that's no MacGuffin!'

Alfred Hitchcock in François Truffaut, 'Hitchcock Interviews',
Touchstone Edition, Simon & Schuster, New York, 1983
(after the MacGuffin story by Angus McPhail)

SANCHEZ CIGARS
NEW YORK'S BEST

Kitchen
Matches

PENLEY

CHES
STRIKE ON BOX

KEEP AWAY FROM CHILDREN

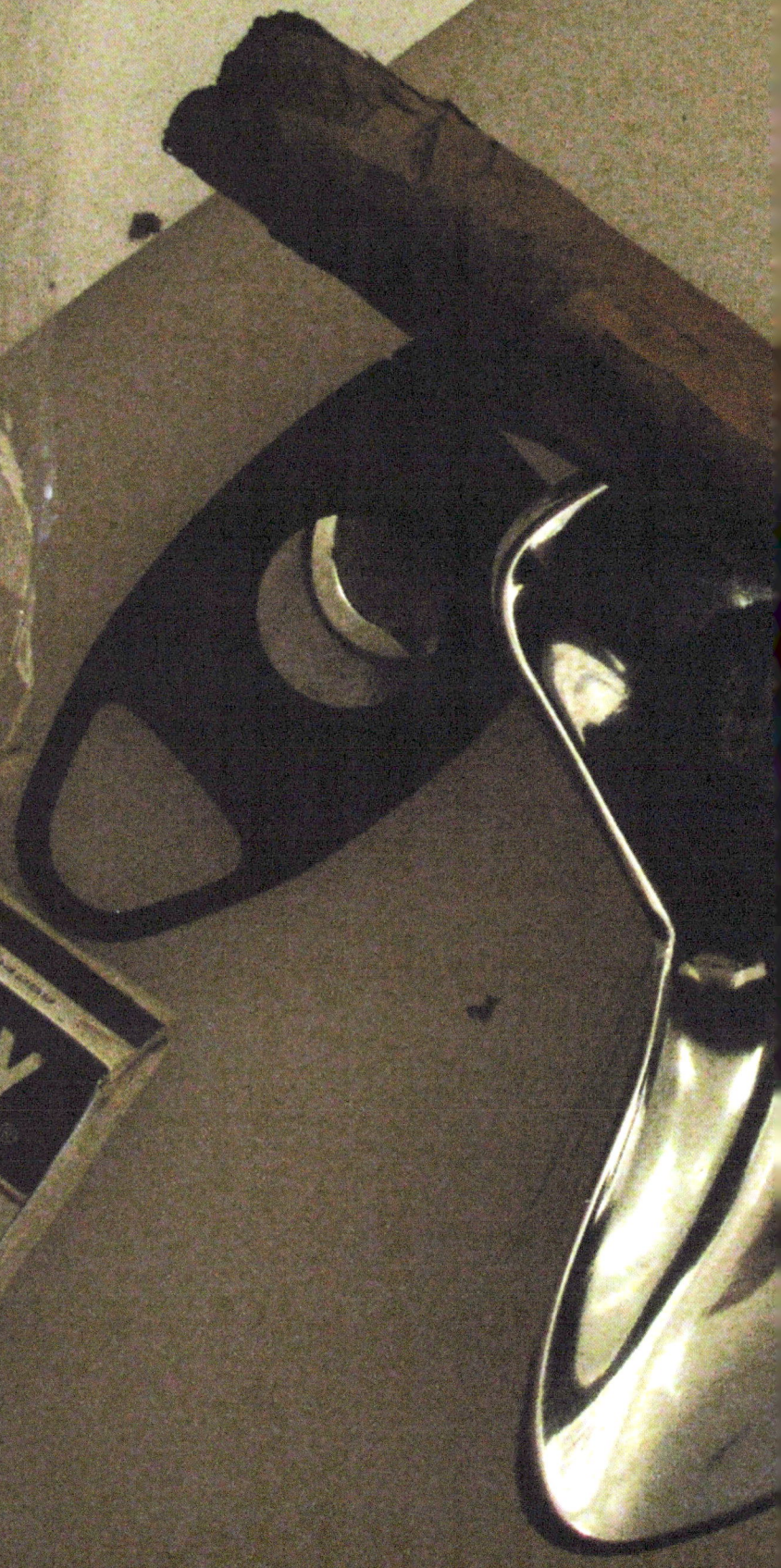

PRODUCT OF CHILE

Hitchcock cameo apperances

Ron Burrage, Hitchcock double, London casting, 2004

H meets H !

Borges: ° 24 Aug 1899 † 14 June 1986

August 25, 1983

I saw by the clock at the little station that it was past eleven. I began walking
through the night toward the hotel. I experienced, as I had at other times in
the past, the resignation and relief we are made to feel by those places most
familiar to us. The wide gate was open; the large country house itself, in
darkness. I went into the vestibule, whose pale mirrors echoed back the
plants of the salon. Strangely, the owner did not recognize me; he turned
the guest register around for me to sign. I picked up the pen chained to the
register stand, dipped it in the brass inkwell, and then, as I leaned over the
open book, there occurred the first of the many surprises the night would
have in store for me—my name, Jorge Luis Borges, had already been written
there, and the ink was not yet dry. *→ Alfred Hitcock*

   "I thought you'd already gone upstairs," the owner said to me. Then he
looked at me more closely and corrected himself: "Oh, I beg your pardon,
sir. You look so much like the other gentleman, but you are younger."

   "What room is he in?" I asked.

   "He asked for Room 19," came the reply.

   It was as I had feared.

   I dropped the pen and hurried up the stairs. Room 19 was on the third
floor; it opened onto a sad, run-down sort of terrace with a park bench and,
as I recall, a railing running around it. It was the hotel's most secluded
room. I tried the door; it opened at my touch. The overhead light still
burned. In the pitiless light, I came face to face with myself. There, in the
narrow iron bed—older, withered, and very pale—lay I, on my back, my
eyes turned up vacantly toward the high plaster moldings of the ceiling.
Then I heard the voice. It was not exactly my own; it was the one I often
hear in my recordings, unpleasant and without modulation.

"How odd," it was saying, "we are two yet we are one. But then nothing is odd in dreams."

"Then . . ." I asked fearfully, "all this is a dream?"

"It is, I am sure, my last dream." He gestured toward the empty bottle on the marble nightstand. "You, however, shall have much to dream, before you come to this night. What date is it for you?"

"I'm not sure," I said, rattled. "But yesterday was my sixty-first birthday."

"When in your waking state you reach this night again, yesterday will have been your eighty-fourth. Today is August 25, 1983."

"So long to wait," I murmured.

"Not for me," he said shortly. "For me, there's almost no time left. At any moment I may die, at any moment I may fade into that which is unknown to me, and still I dream these dreams of my double . . . that tiresome subject I got from Stevenson and mirrors."

I sensed that the evocation of Stevenson's name was a farewell, not some empty stroke of pedantry. I was he, and I understood. It takes more than life's most dramatic moments to make a Shakespeare, hitting upon memorable phrases. To distract him, I said:

"I knew this was going to happen to you. Right here in this hotel, years ago, in one of the rooms below, we began the draft of the story of this suicide."

"Yes," he replied slowly, as though piecing together the memories, "but I don't see the connection. In that draft I bought a one-way ticket for Adrogué,* and when I got to the Hotel Las Delicias I went up to Room 19, the room farthest from all the rest. It was there that I committed suicide."

"That's why I'm here," I said.

"*Here?* We've always been *here.* It's here in this house on Calle Maipú that I am dreaming you. It is here, in this room that belonged to Mother, that I am taking my departure."

". . . that belonged to Mother," I repeated, not wanting to understand. "I am dreaming you in Room 19, on the top floor, next to the rooftop terrace."

"Who is dreaming whom? I know I am dreaming you—I do not know whether you are dreaming me. That hotel in Adrogué was torn down years and years ago—twenty, maybe thirty. Who knows?"

"I am the dreamer," I replied, with a touch of defiance.

"Don't you realize that the first thing to find out is whether there is only one man dreaming, or two men dreaming each other?"

"I am Borges. I saw your name in the register and I came upstairs."

"But I am Borges, and I am dying in a house on Calle Maipú."

There was a silence, and then he said to me:

"Let's try a test. What was the most terrible moment of our life?"

I leaned over him and the two of us spoke at once. I know that neither of us spoke the truth.

A faint smile lit up the aged face. I felt that that smile somehow reflected my own.

"We've lied to each other," he said, "because we feel that we are two, not one. The truth is that we are two yet we are one."

I was beginning to be irritated by this conversation, and I told him so. Then I added: "And you, there in 1983—are you not going to tell me anything about the years I have left?"

"What can I tell you, poor Borges? The misfortunes you are already accustomed to will repeat themselves. You will be left alone in this house. You will touch the books that have no letters and the Swedenborg medallion and the wooden tray with the Federal Cross. Blindness is not darkness; it is a form of solitude. You will return to Iceland."

"Iceland! Sea-girt Iceland!"

"In Rome, you will once more recite the poetry of Keats, whose name, like all men's names, was writ in water."

"I've never been in Rome."

"There are other things. You will write our best poem—an elegy."

"On the death of . . ." I began. I could not bring myself to say the name.

"No. She will outlive you."

We grew silent. Then he went on:

"You will write the book we've dreamed of for so long. In 1979 you will see that your supposed career has been nothing but a series of drafts, miscellaneous drafts, and you will give in to the vain and superstitious temptation to write your great book—the superstition that inflicted upon us Goethe's *Faust*, and *Salammbô*, and *Ulysses*. I filled, incredible to tell, many, many pages."

"And in the end you realized that you had failed."

"Worse. I realized that it was a masterpiece in the most overwhelming sense of the word. My good intentions hadn't lasted beyond the first pages; those that followed held the labyrinths, the knives, the man who thinks he's an image, the reflection that thinks it's real, the tiger that stalks in the night, the battles that are in one's blood, the blind and fatal Juan Muraña, the voice of Macedonio Fernández, the ship made with the fingernails of the dead, Old English repeated in the evening."

"That museum rings a bell," I remarked sarcastically.

"Not to mention false recollections, the doubleness of symbols, the long catalogs, the skilled handling of prosaic reality, the imperfect symmetries that critics so jubilantly discover, the not always apocryphal quotations."

"Did you publish it?"

"I toyed, without conviction, with the melodramatic possibility of destroying the book, perhaps by fire. But I wound up publishing it in Madrid, under a pseudonym. I was taken for a clumsy imitator of Borges—a person who had the defect of not actually being Borges yet of mirroring all the outward appearances of the original."

"I'm not surprised," I said. "Every writer sooner or later becomes his own least intelligent disciple."

"That book was one of the roads that led me to this night. The others . . . The humiliation of old age, the conviction of having already lived each day . . ."

"I will not write that book," I said.

"You will, though. My words, which are now your present, will one day be but the vaguest memory of a dream."

I found myself annoyed by his dogmatic tone, the tone that I myself no doubt use in my classes. I was annoyed by the fact that we resembled each other so much and that he was taking advantage of the impunity lent him by the nearness of death.

"Are you so sure," I said, to get back at him a bit, "that you're going to die?"

"Yes," he replied. "I feel a sort of sweetness and relief I've never felt before. I can't describe it; all words require a shared experience. Why do you seem so annoyed at what I'm saying?"

"Because we're too much like each other. I loathe your face, which is a caricature of mine, I loathe your voice, which is a mockery of mine, I loathe your pathetic syntax, which is my own."

"So do I," he smiled. "Which is why I decided to kill myself."

A bird sang from the garden.

"It's the last one," the other man said.

He motioned me toward him. His hand sought mine. I stepped back; I was afraid the two hands would merge.

"The Stoics teach," he said to me, "that we should not complain of life—the door of the prison is open. I have always understood that; I myself saw life that way, but laziness and cowardice held me back. About twelve days ago, I was giving a lecture in La Plata on Book VI of the *Æneid*. Suddenly, as I was scanning a hexameter, I discovered what my path was to be. I made this decision—and since that moment, I have felt myself invulnerable. You shall one day meet that fate—you shall receive that sudden revelation, in the midst of Latin and Virgil, yet you will have utterly forgotten this curious prophetic dialogue that is taking place in two times and two places. When you next dream it, you shall be who I am, and you shall be my dream."

"I won't forget it—I'm going to write it down tomorrow."

"It will lie in the depths of your memory, beneath the tides of your dreams. When you write it, you will think that you're weaving a tale of fantasy. And it won't be tomorrow, either—it will be many years from now."

He stopped talking; I realized that he had died. In a way, I died with him—in grief I leaned over his pillow, but there was no one there anymore.

I fled the room. Outside, there was no patio, no marble staircase, no great silent house, no eucalyptus trees, no statues, no gazebo in a garden, no fountains, no gate in the fence surrounding the hotel in the town of Adrogué.

Outside awaited other dreams.

Negative Reel

Tom McCarthy

'Show me your belly button,' he said.

Negative Reel

Tom McCarthy

The event I am about to recount to you took place in 1968. I was shooting, on a set which replicated a section of La Guardia airport's arrivals hall, an episode of the type which my audience had already come to expect in each new film: the scene in which I myself make a fleeting appearance. The film, in this case, was my Cold War thriller *Topaz*; I was to be pushed through the arrivals hall in a wheelchair until, encountering the person who had come to greet me, I suddenly arose and strode off with him, able-bodied as a sailor. A cameo, a vignette, no more – and yet I wanted, as so often in my *oeuvre*, to set in the balance those close but troubled neighbours, the miraculous and the fake.

We had allotted ourselves just one morning for the shot: time was thus a constant concern. Two thirds of ours had already elapsed by the time we had mounted a Technicolor camera on a crane and a second on a crab-dolly, positioned lights out of shot behind replica desks, signs and trolleys, plotted the routes of the extras playing pilots, stewardesses, passengers and porters through the slightly-curving corridor (the shot required no fewer than thirty people to pass through it) and filmed a first take. We were about to film a second. My continuity supervisor was taking endless Polaroid photographs to ensure verisimilitude should we choose to cut between the two: meticulously recording positions, angles between people, postures, lengths of cigarettes, whether glasses were worn on faces or pushed up onto foreheads and a hundred other factors that had all to be consistent from one moment to the next. Before we did the second take, I substituted a body-double for myself within the wheelchair so that I could oversee a walk-through of the shot once more: all seemed satisfactory. I was about to re-insert myself into the scene and shoot for real again when the camera-loader informed me that the film stock on one of the cameras had run out. In the spirit of economy, he tried to use every available yard of each reel, and had reached the very end of this one: he would need to reload the camera. I called a twelve-minute break. The period was arbitrary but not random: since we were using twelve-minute reels, I'd acquired the habit of measuring time in twelve-minute chunks.

Wanting to clear my head by removing myself from the set, I decided to use the interval to attend to a small but important task I had to perform. Despite having acquired American citizenship a good decade ago, I'd never presented to the authorities a copy of my mother's birth certificate. This was not absolutely necessary, but in order to speed up my application they had indicated, for the record, that I had made this document available to them, and for my part I had promised to provide them with it retrospectively. It had taken me a remarkably long time to track it down; but on the morning of the shoot I'd received a letter from my solicitor in London stating that he'd finally identified the relevant registry office; and I, fully aware of the time difference between our cities, realised that now would be an opportune moment to place a call to him. I slipped through the cordon blocking the set off from the rest of the studio and walked over to a row of telephone cabins near the security door. Finding them occupied, I seated myself on a bench beside them.

As I waited for one to become free, I experienced an acute sensation of déjà vu. It seemed to me that I had lived this moment before – or, rather, created it before, in one of my own films. In the same instant, I became aware of a man sitting on the bench beside me. I saw his shoes first, then, running my eyes up his legs and torso, recognised a physique very similar to my own. I thought at first that my body-double had followed me to the bench, but, casting my gaze back towards the filming area and seeing him leaning against a wall smoking a cigarette, realised that this man could not be he. I looked at my companion's face: he was twenty-three or four, no more; his cheeks were plump, his full hair black and slick (I lost much of mine in my thirties). As I scrutinised him, he pulled from his pocket a jar of English blueberry preserve which I immediately recognised: it was a brand, long discontinued, that I had used many years ago in my unfinished film *Number Thirteen*, in which a jar of it had served to hide a – well, I can't recall the nature of the object hidden in it and it doesn't really matter what it was; it never does. I gasped in amazement, then spoke to this man.

'Are you American?' I asked him.

'English,' he replied. 'I am employed by Peabody Studios to make a moving picture. Our film set is just over there.' He gestured to another area of the giant studio, lying in the opposite direction from the one in which my set was situated. 'I'm taking a short break, and waiting for a telephone to become free so that I can call my mother.'

'Ah,' I said to him. 'Then your name is Alfred Hitchcock. I, too, am Alfred Hitchcock. We are in Los Angeles. It's 1968, and our mother is dead.'

'No,' he replied, 'we are in London. 'It is 1922, and my mother is very much alive.'

'Look,' I told him. 'I can prove that I am you. We live at number 517 High Road, Leytonstone. The sofa in the lounge is green. The kitchen has red wooden chairs in it, and its cupboard holds a minor but intimate secret.'

'This is a prank,' he said. He looked around him, searching among the studio's passing workers for the joke's orchestrators. Then, turning back to me, he ordered: 'Show me your belly button.'

'Certainly not,' I replied. I, too, had begun to suspect a prank. I also looked around, expecting to find Hildyard or Worseley sniggering behind some column or ladder. But they were nowhere to be seen, and the whole area in which we found ourselves was clearly quite devoid of artifice – beside, of course, the obvious dog-ends of props and parts of stage machinery that lay around awaiting transport to another part of the studio, another set. Our section was entirely neutral, uncontrived: a bench beside a row of phone cabins, nothing more – or rather, quite the opposite, so well constructed as to be entirely without edge or limit, and, for this very reason, terrifying. I felt my own reality slipping away, felt that I risked becoming no more than a character in someone else's film. I decided to accept the situation and to play along with it, aware that a failure to do so could prove catastrophic.

'If this is a film,' I continued, and saw from his nod that he understood my logic as completely as if it were his own, 'then my version of it has a more developed plot. Would you like to hear it?'

'Why not?' he assented.

'Well,' I told him. 'We continue making moving pictures, progressing onto ones with sound. We marry our assistant Alma. We move to America. Our mother dies in 1942. What else? We maintain certain habits, eating at Chasens every day – Claridges when in London. But tell me yourself, how is everyone?'

'Mother is fine,' he said. 'Her back gives her some pain. William continues to run the shop. Nellie is to be married in the spring; the wedding arrangements claim all her attention.'

As he spoke I saw them, clearly as in a film: Mother moving around the house clutching her back, Nellie folding cards and licking envelopes, William busying himself among his produce. There was a pause, then he asked me:

'What of the world?'

'Ah, that,' I responded. 'An iron curtain has descended over Europe.'

'Curtain?' he asked.

'Metaphorically speaking,' I said. 'Russia and America are engaged in a Cold War. England has sided with America. So has France, although her affections seem to vacillate between her two suitors. But none of that is interesting in itself.' I glanced at his jar of blueberry preserve again, and asked him: 'What are you working on?'

He told me of a great project he had in mind. I dismissed it as misguided. We moved on to other subjects. I would like to be able to report that our exchanges contained monumental phrases, summations of the very essence of cinema, or life, or both. But scenes of this importance rarely bring the requisite dialogue along with them. We talked about types of camera, the problem of working with actors, the ceaseless struggles one faced with producers. At one point he ventured that he wanted to use film to develop a new language of experience. I told him:

'Ah, I thought you'd say something like that. In time, though, you'll come to see that cinema merely confirms the old language, showing people what they recognise of themselves: guilt, anxiety, strained family relations, death, guilt, above all guilt...'

C.U. DOG
BARKING
and *running pose*

'Why do you speak like that?' he asked me.

'Speak like what?' I retorted.

'Saying 'Ah' all the time, and talking as though you were delivering some lecture you'd penned earlier.'

'You are right,' I said. 'It is a habit into which I have fallen since developing the mannerism in the telev… in the popular entertainment reels I introduce each week. Off-camera, I find myself imitating my on-screen persona.' I started repeating for him a quip I sometimes delivered during after-dinner speeches, explaining that the only reason I had acquired a large girth was to resemble the actor I had (so my gag ran) hired to play me in my cameo appearances, whereas the real me, whom I no longer resembled, was in fact a slim man more akin in looks to Cary Grant. But the joke seemed, in this situation, not so much inappropriate as redundant, and my speech tailed off. Besides, I could see he wasn't really listening: as far as he was concerned, this whole encounter was about him, not me. Ah, the self-centredness of the young…

He sat in contemplation for a while, then said: 'You mentioned the kitchen cupboard in our flat in Leytonstone. So tell me: what is in it?'

'An item of clothing,' I responded.

'Male or female?' he asked.

'You should know that already,' I retorted.

'Indeed,' he said, 'I do. But I want to know if *you* know.'

'This situation is impossible!' I said. 'Besides, if you were me, you'd lie about its nature, just as I would were I you.'

He thought about this, nodding in agreement. Then, striking off on a new piste, he asked me: 'Have you ever put this situation in a film?'

I told him: 'No. How could I have done? It's happening to me for the first time.'

'Aha!' he said triumphantly. 'If you were really me, it wouldn't be, and you would have used it in a psychological thriller.'

'Then it would have become a plot-line,' I replied, 'and no one would believe it.'

'Who cares what they believe?' he asked. (If I had previously harboured any doubts that this man was myself, this line dispelled them.)

'Perhaps my whole career has been one long avoidance of this moment,' I confided in him. 'A setting of it to film.'

'An avoidance,' he asked, 'or a setting-to-film?'

'Both,' I answered. As I spoke the word, I felt fear surge inside my chest, sharp as a knife. It dawned on me that this might be my own death scene playing itself out: my moment of destiny, my assignation – or assassination. I felt a need to claw the fact of my existence back again, to forcefully assert it. I cast around for a prop, a weapon, and found I'd had one with me the whole time: the small red airline courtesy satchel I'd held on my lap as the nurse pushed my wheelchair through the airport's lobby. On its front, beneath the zip, it bore the letters *TWA* and, beneath these, a slogan: *Flying great in '68!*

'Look!' I said, thrusting it at him. 'Look at the date!'

'That's incredible!' he cried. (I found out afterwards that it was the schoolgirl walking behind my wheelchair and not I who had held the satchel – and who, more-over, had kept hold of it during the whole film-reloading break: I'd never touched it.) 'This is an occurrence for which experience has as yet furnished no explanation!' he continued. 'Now I understand why audiences ran screaming from the theatre the first time the Lumière Brothers showed them footage of an approaching train.'

Despite the tenseness of the situation, I smiled. I've never lost that habit of looking to cinema when I want to understand or express something that's happening. 'Yes,' I told him; 'but the same audiences found it less terrifying when they encountered it a second time. Let's come back to this bench tomorrow, at the same time: this bench in Los Angeles, London, '22, '68, flying great – whatever we may call it.'

He agreed, then said he had to go. I said I had to go as well, as I was needed back on set. He said that so was he. We reaffirmed our commitments to return the next day at the same hour. Each of us knew that he would fail to show up – and, therefore, that the other would not show up either. Neither of us placed our phone call.

This all happened some years ago. I have thought about it a lot since, and think that I have worked out what occurred. The episode was too strange to be real. I was, in that short interval, indeed the subject of a hoax, but only inasmuch as I was, as I suspected, a character in someone else's film. If that prank's architect, that film's director, was indeed a younger version of myself (in which case it cannot be taken for granted that it was actually he whom I met – it could have been a stand-in, a body-double), I had excised it from my memory's filmography as that particular film, like *Number Thirteen*, had been abandoned before its completion. During those twelve minutes, I was in his film – but the film was flawed. It was the red satchel that foiled it: a basic continuity mistake. Because of the mistake, the reel was discarded, never developed. My antagonist showed promise but still had a lot to learn. I wouldn't have made that mistake. That's why I'm still here and he's not. Not yet, anyhow.

Hitchcock is not himself today...

Johan Grimonprez in conversation with Chris Darke

We rented 500 local ducks and sprayed them grey. We started off with chickens but the neck movement gave them away.

'The Making of *The Birds*'
Dialogue on Film: Alfred Hitchcock, American Film Institute, 1972,
in 'Alfred Hitchcock/Interviews', ed. Sidney Gottlieb, University Press
of Mississippi, Jackson, 2003

Hitchcock is not himself today...

JOHAN GRIMONPREZ IN CONVERSATION WITH CHRIS DARKE

Islington, North London, March 2007

Chris Darke Do you realise we're talking only a short distance away from the first film studio Hitchcock ever worked in?

Johan Grimonprez The Gainsborough? Yes, I passed it on the way here.

CD Having been on the trail of Hitchcock for almost four years with this project, you must have the feeling that his shadow is everywhere you go.

JG His shadow was already there before! *Looking for Alfred* grew out of a film I'm still writing, actually – a film about 'happy endings', in which 'Hitchcock' would have had a cameo role in the form of a commercial. It was sort of a reality TV story where a Hitchcock plot is set in motion in order to facilitate product placement. At the time, I was writing with a friend of mine, Daragh Reeves, and from this initial need to look for a Hitchcock double, we arrived at an idea for a Hitchcock casting, and then, in the process, became more and more interested in Hitchcock's cameo appearances in his films. We took the idea to Steven Bode at Film and Video Umbrella and he really liked it. And since then it's grown and grown…

CD One of the most noticeable things about *Looking for Alfred*, apart from its highly cinematic aesthetic and its attention to detail, is the extent to which you document so many of the stages of the film-making process.

JG It started off with the castings, which were all documented, not only on video, but also photographed extensively. Later on, during the actual shoot in the Palais des Beaux-Arts in Brussels, I had two people videotaping the whole thing because I specifically wanted to highlight the process of making the work. Not only were we looking for a Hitchcock double, but the idea of having the project itself double – and then doubling and doubling further – was there from the very beginning. I had a plot written with Hitchcock meeting Hitchcock that was based around the idea of two cameo appearances colliding: the cameo from *Stage Fright* (1950), where Hitchcock glances over his shoulder, and the cameo from *Foreign Correspondent* (1940), where he is seen passing by in the street reading a newspaper. I had those two key images almost as emblems, but, since so many of his cameo appearances are not only brief but silent, there was also always a desire to capture something of his language, his distinctive phrasing and vocabulary.

CD   Although you sample elements of Hitchcock's musical scores in *Looking for Alfred*, the only piece of spoken word comes when a Hitchcock impersonator (Mark Perry) retells the famous explanation of the 'MacGuffin' Hitchcock gave in an interview with François Truffaut.

JG   I've read three, four, maybe five versions of the 'MacGuffin' story in several Hitchcock interviews where he tells an almost but not quite identical anecdote about two guys who meet on a train. One asks the other: 'What's that thing you're carrying in the luggage rack?' and he says 'That's a MacGuffin'. The other guy asks, 'What's a MacGuffin?' and the reply is: 'It's a device to trap lions in the Scottish Highlands.' At which point the other guy says: 'But there are no lions in the Scottish Highlands'. *'That's* a MacGuffin,' comes the reply.

CD   'That's *no* MacGuffin', surely.

JG   No, there are *two* versions! Even the people who came for the castings mixed up the two. It *is* a 'MacGuffin' because a 'MacGuffin' is *no* 'MacGuffin'.

CD   In the interviews with Truffaut, Hitchcock speaks at length about its inherent meaninglessness. Among other things, he says – in a delightfully paradoxical way – 'the main thing I've learned over the years is that the MacGuffin is nothing. I'm convinced of this, but I find it very difficult to prove it to others.' It seems to me that, for your purposes, the MacGuffin is not quite nothing…

JG   For Hitchcock, it's the thing that greases the wheels of suspense. It sets the story in motion: a device to start the story-telling process, to make people curious. With *Looking For Alfred*, it was the same. Although we never found the 'Alfred' we were looking for, the pursuit of him led us to other things. Even in *not* finding what, in the end, turns out to have been a MacGuffin, you arrive at another story…

This was vividly brought home to me shortly after the London casting, where I met Ron Burrage, who's been a professional Hitchcock lookalike for at least

It has been whispered about that I hate television commercials. I love them.

Hitchcock's After Dinner Speech

After sixty seconds, I shall turn the commercial into an Alfred Hitchcock.

Alfred Hitchcock Presents,
Series 3, Episode 85

You see, crime doesn't pay. Not even on television. You must have a sponsor.

AHP S1 E1

We slowly turn our eyes back to the charms of television advertising and the lyrical chant of our sponsor's message.

AHP S1 E2

20 years. When I looked at the footage of Ron afterwards, it was eerie and uncanny to see what I began to believe was our perfect Hitchcock double. But then, just when everything was in place, and we were ready to shoot, our main protagonist, Ron, had to go into hospital…

CD You had to get a double for the double…

JG I asked myself 'How can I solve this?' It was a spontaneous solution to go for the complete opposite, our Chinese Hitchcock lookalike, Bruce Ho. It turned out to be a happy accident. We subsequently integrated some footage of Ron into the film, but since so much was missing, I felt I needed to visit him again and I came to London to interview him. This subsequent footage forms a major part of a further development of *Looking for Alfred,* a project called *Double Take.* In a way, I'm aware that I'm continuing to look for something I haven't quite found (and maybe never can), almost as if Hitchcock himself has become our MacGuffin.

CD One of the things you find in your search is that Hitchcock *is* cinema, or cinema at a certain moment in its history, when first confronted by television. The challenge of television was one that Hitchcock took on in a variety of ways: fronting, in a markedly sardonic fashion, his own TV series, *Alfred Hitchcock Presents,* as well as adopting TV production methods (short schedule, small crew, black-and-white) to make *Psycho,* for example.

JG Indeed, but I'd add that Hitchcock had already made a number of similar transitions: the change from silent to sound cinema, from black and white to colour, and also the change from Britain to Hollywood. At the height of his career in the mid-Fifties, he was becoming acutely aware of the challenge of television… that's why *The Birds* is a pivotal point, it reflects the ideology of that particular period, with television – just like the birds themselves – about to invade the home; at a moment when cinema had to redefine itself, losing its audience to television.

CD Given the role that doubles and doubling play in *Psycho* and *Vertigo* why choose *The Birds* as your central Hitchcock work?

JG *The Birds* has generated every possible contradictory interpretation by Hitchcock scholars: the birds embody the tensions between the characters, they're a metaphor for Melanie's sexuality or the repressed anxiety of the mother,

You know, I believe commercials are improving every day. Next week we hope to have another one, equally fascinating and if time permits, we shall bring you another story.

AHP S1 E10

It seems to me that television is exactly like a gun. Your enjoyment of it is determined by which side of it you're on.

AHP S1 E39

When your heart stops yearning, keep your taillight burning. Now for the thumbscrews and the rack. Endure it please for I'll be back.

AHP S2 E67

Erik Grimonprez, Hitchcock double

…anyone touching the channel selector to change programs, gets a nasty shock. We rather hope it will improve the loyalty of our viewers. [BANG!] There goes another one. It's no trifling matter. 25,000 volts leaves them crisp as bacon.

AHP S2 E70

I do wish we had longer commercials. They are so short that one must be very agile to get to the kitchen and back.

AHP S3 E98

If used in large quantities, one of these can bore a person to death.

AHP S3 E87

I get the distinct impression they're trying to sell something.

AHP S3 E95

etc. But, like the MacGuffin, they refuse interpretation. I went for *The Birds* to allude to Hitchcock's ambivalent relationship with television and, by way of a detour, to lead back to the theme of the double – in particular, television as cinema's 'double'. I came across an essay by Angelo Restivo in which he asks the interesting question: 'Why does nobody switch on the TV set in *The Birds*?' For me, the first thing you'd do when you're trapped in a house with some kind of catastrophe going on outside would be to turn on the TV! The implication is that the model community of Bodega Bay is being invaded by birds in the same way that television invades suburbia, turning the American nuclear family into happy consumers; in the process (and this was the concern for filmmakers like Hitchcock) displacing people's relationship with the cinema. In Hitchcock's words: 'TV brought murder into the American household, where it always belonged.'

It is interesting that when Hitchcock chooses to cross over to television, in the form of *Alfred Hitchcock Presents*, he goes out of his way to poke fun at TV: pointing out the extent to which the medium is itself infected by advertising, hijacked by the commercial break. Although he made his name in the cinema, *Alfred Hitchcock Presents*, and its successor, *The Alfred Hitchcock Hour*, were equally responsible for turning Hitchcock into a household figure: the belly, the protruding lip, the double chin… Over a period of around ten years, Hitchcock hosted about 370 episodes of his TV series. He introduced each and every one, as he said 'to lay his customary one-minute egg'; basically to berate the sponsors, while announcing the commercial with a large dose of sardonic humour. This adds up to about 360 minutes of Hitchcock performances which have hardly been examined at all in Film Studies, although they constitute an essential part of what Hitchcock was about: the biggest television prankster.

CD It strikes me that Hitchcock colonised our childhood imagination: yours, mine, and that of the New Wave directors in 1950s Paris, to mention only a few of his many victims! How old were you when you saw your first Hitchcock? Was it in a cinema or on TV? When did you realise he was more than just another filmmaker?

JG As a little kid, I remember a paperback from my Dad's bookshelves. On the cover was a man who looked very much like my Dad: double chin, bald head, a protruding lip puffing a cigar, a big belly with the pants too high. I guess that must have been my first confrontation with the image of Hitchcock, only to learn later there's more than just my Dad to Hitchcock's image. (Funnily enough, as we were casting in Belgium, I invited my Dad along, never thinking he would make it into the film but he ended up restaging Hitchcock's cameo from *Strangers on a Train* (1951), carrying a double bass, while picking up the bowler hat that rolls into shot.)

As for Hitchcock's films, I didn't discover them in the cinema. We're a generation who discovered his legacy second hand, either through re-runs on television or through video and DVD (the 'doubling' of his films, as it were). The very first time I saw a cinema screening of *Vertigo*, reels two and three were projected in the wrong order which meant I saw the point where Madeleine had changed in to Judy before I should have, which gave the plot a very disconcerting and bizarre angle. But this is actually very similar to how with DVD you can skip scenes, and jump back and forth through the storyline.

CD In *Looking for Alfred*, you also jump backwards and forwards combining cameo appearances from Hitchcock films from completely different eras. Tell me a little more about what attracted you to these cameos.

JG Hitchcock loved to play hide-and-seek with himself, as well as with the audience. 'Spot the director', as Thomas Leitch calls it. Or, in the words of Raymond Bellour, Hitchcock, by making a cameo, 'inscribed himself in the films' chain of fantasy.' To invoke a more literary model, it's a classic case of the storyteller mirroring himself in the story. The cameos started when he ran out of extras on the set of his directorial debut, *The Lodger*, and to save money he took on the role himself. Later on, they became a kind of superstitious ritual that he enacted in each of his films. Often, he's a casual passer-by or a fellow traveller who pops up at an airport, in a train, in a street or a hotel lobby, and his appearance, when it arrives, frequently foreshadows a fateful decision or a turning point in the story. In *Strangers on a Train*, for example, Hitchcock boards the train where the two strangers are about to exchange murders. The larger and more devoted his audience became, however, the more familiar they were with both Hitchcock's image and the regular nature of his walk-on appearances. Because of this, the cameos were in danger of turning into a gag that distracted from the story, and he decided to get them out of the way as early as possible in a film. Think of *North by Northwest* (1959) for example, when he misses the bus just before his name appears in the credits. We actually replayed this cameo during the L.A. casting, when we tried to miss the bus with three of the cast of Hitchcocks on Wilshire Boulevard right in front of the casting building (just before we had a break for the Hitchcock dinner, to which I invited all the callbacks.)

…but we must first have our sponsor's product. Stuffed in the suffocating sack of commercialism and drowned in a sea of adjectives.
AHP S3 E102

And tonight as a special attraction we shall present some television commercials. I knew you'd like that. They will be injected at various points during our picture to keep you from getting too engrossed in the story. I understand they're very good at relieving tensions, and furnishing comic relief.
AHP S3 E112

I think I shall take this opportunity to walk my dog.
AHP S4 E123

Now please, no screams.
AHP S4 E144

CD In *Looking for Alfred*, you address Hitchcock's cameo appearances, while in your new, extended version of the project, *Double Take*, you look more closely at his TV persona. One of the things you seem to want to do, with the cameos at least, is to make them come alive again through of one of the stranger out-growths of celebrity culture, the celebrity impersonator. Do you call on this as a way of casting a light on the Hitchcock persona or on his relationship with cinema and television?

JG The fact that Hitchcock always wore a suit, for example, was a disguise to hide his shyness and unease with his own body. As the 'cavalier of the macabre', as he came to be called, he would transform this into a persona that became part and parcel of his practical jokes. And then later, in his appearances on TV, he clearly, and very cleverly, played with doubles of that persona. He would work the strings of a life-size lookalike marionette, walk off with his own wax head under his arm (which later ended up in his wife's fridge as a prank), dress as a woman or a dog. He'd be mistaken for himself, meet his stand-in, or often appear as his own brother explaining that Alfred is nowhere to be found... The funniest example of all is when Hitchcock himself is disqualified in the first round of a Hitchcock lookalike contest, with him playing three other lookalikes introducing his show!

CD But my point is that when you start to deal with the celebrity lookalike as double don't you risk losing what's crucial to Borges, Dostoyevsky and Poe – just as it is to José Saramago's recent novel 'The Double' – the underpinning of existential angst that's in all those classic narratives of the double? After all, a *doppelgänger* narrative is meant to make you feel that the ground beneath your feet is a bit uncertain, that the world is a little strange.

JG Absolutely. Seeing one's own *doppelgänger* is usually depicted as a harbinger of bad luck, and it's often a premonition of death. Also, strangely, the double is believed to have no reflection in the mirror. Because he performs the protagonist's actions in advance, he *is* the mirror that eventually takes over. It's like the evil twins narrative with Bart and Hugo Simpson: the double plays the same part as the hero but from the evil angle. The template for the film I'm working on at the moment, *Double Take*, is based on a similar plot to that, where a Hitchcock *doppelgänger* takes over the host's role to present the episode *The Case of Mr Pelham*, which is itself reminiscent of Edgar Allen Poe's story of mistaken identity, 'William Wilson', who is dogged by his counterpart. The narration of *Double Take* is inspired by the Borges novella, 'The Other', where

Man, I've changed my mind. That was the greatest. The story may be unhip, but those crazy commercials are pure poetry. They deserve better treatment.

AHP S4 E147

Frankly, I have now lost my appetite completely.

AHP S5 E164

I shall be in orbit during the next minute so I'm afraid I shall miss the commercial.

AHP S5 E166

I realise you have already had two commercials, but why not have one more for the road?

AHP S5 E171

the author encounters his older self. And that, in turn refers to Dostoyevsky's 'The Double'. It's interesting to note that there are two versions. The text has its own double! Borges wrote a later version of that text dated '25 August 1983'. It's this later version that is included in the *Double Take* project and also featured here in the book, where the novelist Tom McCarthy reworked the earlier version. In our story, however, it's Hitchcock who bumps into Hitchcock, an allusion to his cameo appearances in his films, where Hitchcock, the storyteller, doubles himself in his own stories.

CD   In both *Looking for Alfred* and *Double Take* you examine the function of iconography in Hitchcock. There are everyday objects and details that are deadly (lethal cups of tea and coffee), or malign (sparrows that kill!), or that act as a form of disguise, such as the bowler hat, an affectation that Hitchcock shared with Magritte.

JG   I could almost imagine Magritte and Hitchcock disguised as Laurel and Hardy appearing from around the corner in the Palais des Beaux-Arts in Brussels! Or, as the famous double act Thomson & Thompson, the Belgian bowler-hatted detectives from the *Tintin* books. Thomson & Thompson are utterly Belgian. There's something about their doubleness that rings so true for a country that's embedded in the cultural schizophrenia of two languages living side by side; one constantly translating or repeating the other and never taking it seriously. Everything has to be duplicated or translated. You're forced always to do things twice, just like Thomson & Thompson (and our doubled governing institutions, the Flemish and the Walloon). Before you even start talking, you first have to decide which language you'll choose. So misunderstanding becomes culture, the poetry of misinterpretation. And words and things start to disconnect.

Belgian reality comes subtitled. Simply in the act of buying milk and reading the labels you're immediately enmeshed in translating into another language. To always be confronted with the other side of things sharpens the sense of irony. Most television programmes and films are subtitled (a big chunk of our television programmes were always imported). This is second nature so, as a kid, you think the whole world is subtitled. You grow up translating the world. This is so much part of Magritte's language paintings, as well. He subtitles his pipe with 'pipe' and 'not a pipe'. It's always already something else. It's maybe this irony that leads to a particular variation of surrealism. 'Today there were two Mondays,' writes Magritte. 'To speak is to commit tautologies,' says Borges.

I'm not sure what to say. That last commercial left me completely underwhelmed.

AHP S5 E176

And now for the part of the programme you have all been waiting for.

AHP S1 E5

There now, that really held you in suspense, didn't it?

AHP S1 E7

And now for those of you who are accustomed to enjoying television, here is something that is also refreshingly different, after which I'll be back.

AHP S5 E177

Magritte was only a year older then Hitchcock. Both were born in the very late 1890s, which coincided with the Lumiére brothers projecting their first film. The idea of blurring boundaries between what is the same and nearly exactly the same – but not quite – is very much a recurrent theme in both of their work. For Hitchcock, it was a plot device in a lot of his films. Think of Madeleine in *Vertigo*, for example. For Magritte, *doppelgängers* often appear. I was interested in this as a way of exploring mistaken identity. The uncanny feeling that in a situation, something, or someone, looks exactly the same as another but somehow is not and hence is totally displaced. It creates unease and a sense of anxiety that both prefigures impending disaster but, precisely because of this, also reveals a glimpse of the sublime. Both admired the work of de Chirico and Poe, masters of what Freud called 'the uncanny'.

Like all saboteurs, Hitchcock and Magritte avoided detection by dressing inconspicuously in their everyday suits as a bourgeois disguise but in their work they were both out to disrupt the apparatus of bourgeois reality – like Magritte's favourite anti-hero Fantômas, a man of infinite disguises who always manages to outwit the police. For Magritte, like Hitchcock, the bowler hat is a prop to conceal one's identity beneath the guise of everyday life, just as Hitchcock had infinite disguises in his television series (usually accompanied with an oversized prop, as in Magritte's paintings).

CD   This is the idea of Hitchcock as a 'double agent' that you pick up on from Thomas Elsaesser who's written that there was a time when Hitchcock was a 'dandy' in the sense of a particular kind of European, aestheticised subversion. But when he goes to America he takes on the guise of what Elsaesser calls the 'saltimbanque', a buffoon, a performer…

JG   Yeah, wearing a suit in the middle of the Californian summer and never taking it off…

CD   But is it the case that one retrospectively finds in Hitchcock the image one wants to find? Such as the image of the subversive artist working in the heart of Hollywood. Do you feel sure that he was as subversive as these retrospective assessments cast him?

JG   No, there's a complete bourgeois pose, as with Magritte. Nonetheless, in the work itself he absolutely pushes the language of cinema and now, in retrospect, those things have become part of our common everyday language.

If you have tuned in to hear me make snide remarks about an innocent sponsor, you are doomed to disappointment. I am proud to say, I have resolved my antagonisms and have become completely sponsor-orientated. I have met our new sponsor and find him [*a halo appears above his head*] to be agreeable, charming, witty, honest, sincere, intelligent, dependable, trustworthy, loyal, brave, clean and reverent. Tonight's show is entitled 'Mrs. Bixby and the Colonel's Coat'. But first, unfortunately, we have one of those… [*halo disappears*], but first fortunately, we have one of those intelligent, amusing, dignified, provocative, brilliantly conceived, [*gives an expression of disgust*] but painfully short commercials.

AHP S6 E192

Of course, he was limited by the constraints of the time, and of working for a major studio, but still he was trying to stretch the agenda and the vocabulary. We have to be very specific about which period in his career we're talking about. I certainly feel he takes on a number of taboos in his television work. The criminal often gets away with the crime; and Hitchcock himself, of course, fires a number of shots at the programme's sponsor. And then I think of *North by Northwest* – a genius film, pre-James Bond, that set the genre, but in which the politics are so right wing, re-inscribing itself in the Cold War…

CD In *Looking for Alfred* and *Double Take* you're dealing with Hitchcock as representative of cinema at a moment when it's having to deal with the challenge from TV, a transitional moment. I'm wondering what you think about the fact that you're doing this at a moment when cinema is undergoing a further mutation relative to digitalisation and when the gallery and the museum have become sites where cinema – quite often through the figure of Hitchcock – becomes if not personified then memorialised?

JG With the invention of photography, the portrait within painting had to be redefined. Painting still exists but photography is now fully recognised as an art form. With the whole digital revolution there's now a way, with Final Cut Pro, to edit very quickly. These digital tools mean that the museum has to redefine itself and Hitchcock and, to a degree, the whole archive of film history, are part of that. There's also a whole shift going on within the art world in terms of its own relationship to new media, to web design etc. Hitchcock pops up everywhere. For me, though, it's a second-degree question; something I shy away from. I would rather say 'OK, let's look at *The Simpsons*'. The fact that there are a couple of Hitchcock spoofs on *The Simpsons* (Hitchcock walking his two dogs Geoffrey and Stanley just like his cameo in *The Birds*; Bart playing James Stewart, with the big camera, investigating a murder among his neighbours) is as interesting a phenomenon to me as Hitchcock's recent appearance in galleries and museums.

The gallery is one part of all of this, I think, but it's bigger than that. It has to do with a larger shift brought about by digital technology where images are increasingly available in so many different ways. We already mentioned how our generation grew up more with television than cinema. DVD makes Hitchcock even more readily available, to the point where you needn't ever have to go to the cinema. The way we relate to the world through its double, through its representation, changed the way we plugged into reality. There's an echo in this of the themes I explored in *Dial H-I-S-T-O-R-Y*; a sense of having been born at

If you think watching a commercial is tiring, you should try cleaning up afterwards.
AHP E191

As for my present mood, will it out-last the final commercial? You shall see in a moment.
AHP S6 E192

Now a stranger approacheth to tell us what to do with those extra farthings.
AHP S6 E194

I see another commercial is coming up. It's amazing what you see when you don't have a gun.
AHP S6 E199

In one of his routines as an amateur magician, Dad wanted to perform the 'rabbit out of the hat' trick but, alas, Kamiel, our rabbit, had eaten too much and was simply too fat to make it through the hole on the side of the hat.

Double Take, Johan Grimonprez

Double Take, Johan Grimonprez

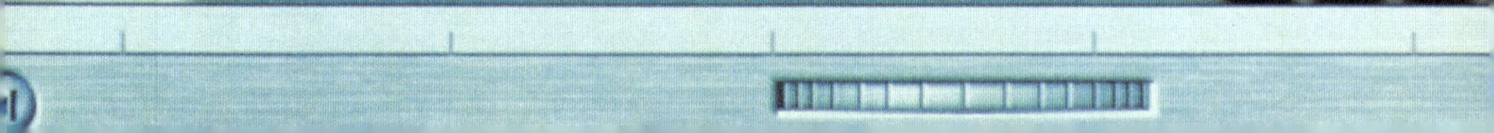

Nom	▼	Début des donné
📁 archives		
▶ 📁 HITCH MOVIES		
▶ 📁 pub 70		
▶ 📁 HITCHCOCK PRESENTS		
▶ 📁 HITCHCOCK PRESENTS season 2		
▶ 📁 HITCHCOCK HOUR		
▶ 📁 9–11		
▶ 📁 baisers		
▶ 📁 caméos		
▶ 📁 clips remote control		
▶ 📁 divers		
🎞 H cannes+Itw fr.mov		00:00:00:00
🎞 H Itw London Theater.mov		00:00:00:00
▶ 📁 sélect plans films		
▶ 📁 the end hitch		
▶ 📁 trailers		
📁 imports divers		
📁 K7 extra		
📁 ron		
📁 rushes BXL		
📁 rushes casting		
📁 rushes LFA		
📁 rushes Test		
📁 SEQ DOUBLE TAKE dvd		
📁 sequences 2004		
📁 sequences 2006		
▼ 📁 THEMES		
🎬 ascenseur		01:00:00:00

Timeline : SEQ FINAL

SEQ FINAL 24 nov | SEQ FINAL 30 nov | SEQ DOUBLE TAKE dvd nov30 – f | Hitch Hour sélect

| TR ▾ | 01:31:16:17 | 00:00 | 01:05 00:00 | 01:10:00:00 | 01:15:00:0 |

v1 (V4)
(V3)
(V2)
(V1)   voic Ifa I T

birdbirds VOB.ff md   Ifa wif

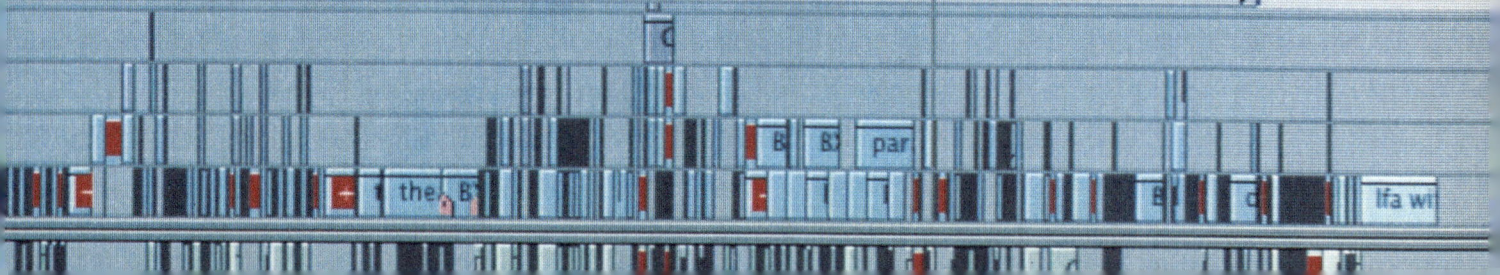

a certain moment in time, in 1962 (the year of the making of *The Birds!*), when the shift from cinemas to television was fully happening and Hollywood had to redefine itself.

CD *Dial H-I-S-T-O-R-Y* (a film that traces the history of airplane hijacking and with that the recent history of news media), raises an interesting question regarding the way you work. The length of time over which you tend to develop a project seems to allow you to go deeper into an idea or obsession and uncover connections that other more superficial appraisals of the subject frequently miss. *Dial H-I-S-T-O-R-Y,* and the way you're dealing with Hitchcock, could be described as a kind of 'media archaeology'. You're interested in the way that media mutate and the ways that mass perception changes.

JG It's also a way of questioning myself as an artist. It's present in *Dial H-I-S-T-O-R-Y,* in the use of Don Delillo's 'Mao 2' where the writer is in dialogue with a terrorist and in which the book contends that the terrorist has taken over the role of the writer in terms of the range of his influence over what Delillo calls 'the inner life of the culture'. Where does he stand? It's a way to break open those boundaries and ask where, as an artist, do you stand politically and relative to the mainstream. It's a way of opening up the agenda rather than trying to reduce it.

I do take a lot of time over each of my works! I like to chew the cud like a cow! But working in this way helps me see parallels and continuities in them. There is a metaphor of birds-as-planes that carries over from *Dial H-I-S-T-O-R-Y* to the present work on Hitchcock, but which goes back all the way to a much earlier piece like *Kobarweng, or Where is Your Helicopter?*, which traces the aftershocks of the first encounter between a group of New Guinean villagers, and the scientists who first arrived, by aircraft, in uncharted territory (*Kobarweng* translated literally, means 'language' of 'the airplane'.)

It also allows me to pull in a number of other reference-points, such as Slavoj Žižek's description of the 9/11 attacks as a real-life version of *The Birds*. For Žižek, 9/11 is the ultimate Hitchcockian threat that suddenly appears out of nowhere. He's thinking specifically of the scene when Melanie (Tippi Hedren) approaches the Bodega Bay pier in a small boat, and a single seagull, first perceived as an indistinguishable dark blot, unexpectedly swoops down and gashes her forehead; an image that is strikingly similar to the plane hitting the second World Trade Centre tower.

And speaking of sell, we have had complaints that our sponsor's sell is too soft, viewers have the feeling something is being left out of the commercials. For them, here is the uncensored, uncooked version.
AHP S6 E200

I don't mind you leaving the room during the commercial, but I expect you to be in your seats for my parts of the programme.
AHP S6 E202

But first, something from which there is no escape.
AHP S6 E208

Our world is packed with an abundance of images that constantly bombard us, and inevitably much of our reality today is filtered through cinema and media imagery. In that respect, 9/11 brought fiction back to haunt us as reality – that eerie sense that we've seen these things before; that things are doubled. There's an echo here of what Thomas Elsaesser, in his essay in this publication, refers to as an 'ontological shift', in which Hollywood seems to run ahead of the facts. It's a direction I'm looking to explore further in *Double Take*.

CD   We should make it clear that *Double Take* is a project that doesn't yet exist as a finished work and is very different to the gallery film of *Looking For Alfred*.

JG   It's a 'double take' on the whole project. You look at it twice. There are elements from the *Looking for Alfred* film, and lots more from the casting material. There is the *doppelgänger* plot that I mentioned above in relation to Hitchcock's use of a double persona on *Alfred Hitchcock Presents*. And, in relation to that, there's a much greater spotlight on Ron Burrage. I believe that Hitchcock would have loved to encounter himself. And in that sense, Ron was a big part of pushing this project into something else. Here's someone from a totally different world, whose connection with a Hollywood icon, through circumstances not entirely of his making, has become his life. It seemed an interesting twist of fate to start exploring. For years, Ron impersonated Hitchcock in everything from Robert Lepage's *Le Confessionnal* (1995), itself a remake, to soap and shampoo commercials, to making guest appearances in music videos for (the rock group) Oasis, while also introducing *Hitchcock Presents* on Italian television, or starring as his double in a Japanese documentary about the life of the master…

There was more to the resemblance than met the eye. As well as Hitchcock's mannerisms, Ron seems to have adopted much of Hitchcock's persona, including his fondness for pranks. In one of those great coincidences, Ron actually shares his birthday (August 13) with Hitchcock. The first time he told me this, he actually said 'Our birthday', and when pressed on this, he joked: 'The Queen would say 'We are not amused'. '*We*'. 'That is, Alfred and me.' The Hitchcock centenary (1999) was a busy time for Ron. Among the many tribute events that year, Ron attended the launch of the newly restored print of *The Birds* in Locarno, at which Tippi Hedren, after all her history with Hitchcock, was introduced to the audience by his *doppelgänger*, Ron. In a further (Hitchcockian) twist, the event actually took place on August 13, with Ron not only filling in for the master, but literally taking over his role, and cutting his and Hitchcock's 100th birthday cake on stage.

Tonight we have fried chicken, cold apple pie, potato salad, a story entitled 'The Land Lady' and one fast frozen commercial. [*eats a chicken leg*]

AHP S6 E210

This man's record is spotless. After all, boring people to death is not yet a criminal offence.

AHP S6 E226

But before we show you the story, we want to test your reflexes with this commercial. If on seeing it, you have the impulse to leave the room, you are absolutely normal.

AHP S7 E236

This phenomenon of a doubling of the personality – a recurring theme in Hitchcock's films – appears to have affected his lookalike. He is the 'Wrong Man', displaced by his uncanny likeness to someone else. To an extent, he has interiorised this identity and blurred the lines between his reality and Hollywood celebrity.

CD   I understand he doesn't particularly like H's films.

JG   He likes opera! He and his partner, who unfortunately passed away last year, and who was also employed for a while as the lookalike of a French actor, used to go to the opera in any spare time that they had. Ron was a flight attendant for British Airways, and one day, by strange twist of fate, found himself serving tea for Ingrid Bergman. Before that he worked in London at Claridge's and the Savoy; places that Hitchcock frequented whenever he was back over from Hollywood. But here Ron was at the opposite end of the food chain: a waiter serving Cary Grant, James Mason, and amongst others, Laurel and Hardy. Next time, I promised to turn things around and take him for lunch at Claridges for our next *rendez-vous*…

But for the moment we've only had coffee! The version of *Double Take* I'm working on starts with a 'Folgers' coffee commercial and then jumps to the cup of coffee we share with Ron at his home. And hovering in the background, of course, is Hitchcock's famous poisoned coffee cup, his way of spiking the ritual products of the commercial break…

CD   In *The Birds*, the setting of Bodega Bay functions as this new utopia of suburban domesticity and, in his essay on the film, Angelo Restivo suggests that this world somehow coheres around the ritual of drinking tea and coffee…

JG   The screenwriter of *The Birds*, Evan Hunter, wanted to do something with the relationship between Melanie and the mother that would libidinise the plot. So there's a certain tension beneath that suburban setting, a love story underneath the tea ritual. And remember, too, how the birds zoom in on the teacups…

Hitchcock treats the cup of coffee with deserved suspicion, and is just as ambivalent about his female characters. He often has strong female leads who are agents of dangerous sexuality, set against a figure of male hysteria, a man who is often doubled, or trapped in a case of mistaken identity, whose fear of

I want to apologise for the lack of bloodshed on tonight's programme. We should try to do better next time. However, if all you wishes something to make your blood run cold, we have commercials to do that.
AHP S7 E244

What has no legs, is a bit thick, definitely does not fly and is one minute long.
AHP S7 E246

An item for which I have a passion. Frankly, I like them because I feel so wonderful when they're over.
AHP S7 E249

The next minute promises to be rather painful.
AHP S7 E250

intimacy (or death), like Hitchcock's, is projected back onto the female character, as a way to try to contain her, or poison her (*Notorious* and *Suspicion*). However, in *Looking for Alfred* the tables are turned. Instead of the female protagonist being trapped and poisoned, she brings the poisoned cup to Hitchcock. She not only poisons him but, instead of being attacked by the birds, she devours the bird.

I occasionally step out for a breath of air during the commercial, but there are limits to what even a company man can endure.

AHP S7 E252

Restivo relates how coffee houses were an integral part of early democratic culture, and how these places of conversation and discussion were increasingly replaced by television giving us the commercial break (instead of the coffee break.) It's interesting how the characters in *The Birds* fail to forge social links, and by extension a public sphere is lost to consumer culture (and its repressed undercurrent: the catastrophe). But here, of course, the birds – as harbingers of catastrophe – shatter the coffee cups, invade the world of domestic bliss! It's maybe not a coincidence that 1963, the year of *The Birds,* was also the year when the Federal Communications Commission limited the amount of advertising on radio and television!

And speaking of money, I shall be back in a moment.

AHP S7 E264

I haven't yet fully developed how I'm going to integrate all this into *Double Take,* but it definitely ties back into the idea of the commercial break and the happy ending. Although the growing popularity of television in the 1960s didn't mean the end of cinema, it did mark the end of 'The End'. By which I mean that the words themselves went out of fashion, losing out to endless credits. *The Birds* is the first Hitchcock film not to feature 'The End'. He leaves it deliberately open-ended (as if waiting for the next episode or instalment), and then dispenses with 'The End' in all of his subsequent films. To an extent, you could say that television has redefined what an 'end' is all about. It gave us ever-lasting TV serials with postponed endings, coached us in the obsessive behaviour of live 'round the clock' news reports, not to mention 'zapping' during the commercial break. What does that leave us with? Essentially, with an image without end… And isn't it funny how it was Hitchcock, in the early days of television, who urged us to zap away from those 'deadly boring commercials'?

Do not attempt to leave your living room or to change channels. Any attempt to defect will be dealt with harshly.

Alfred Hitchcock Hour S1 E5

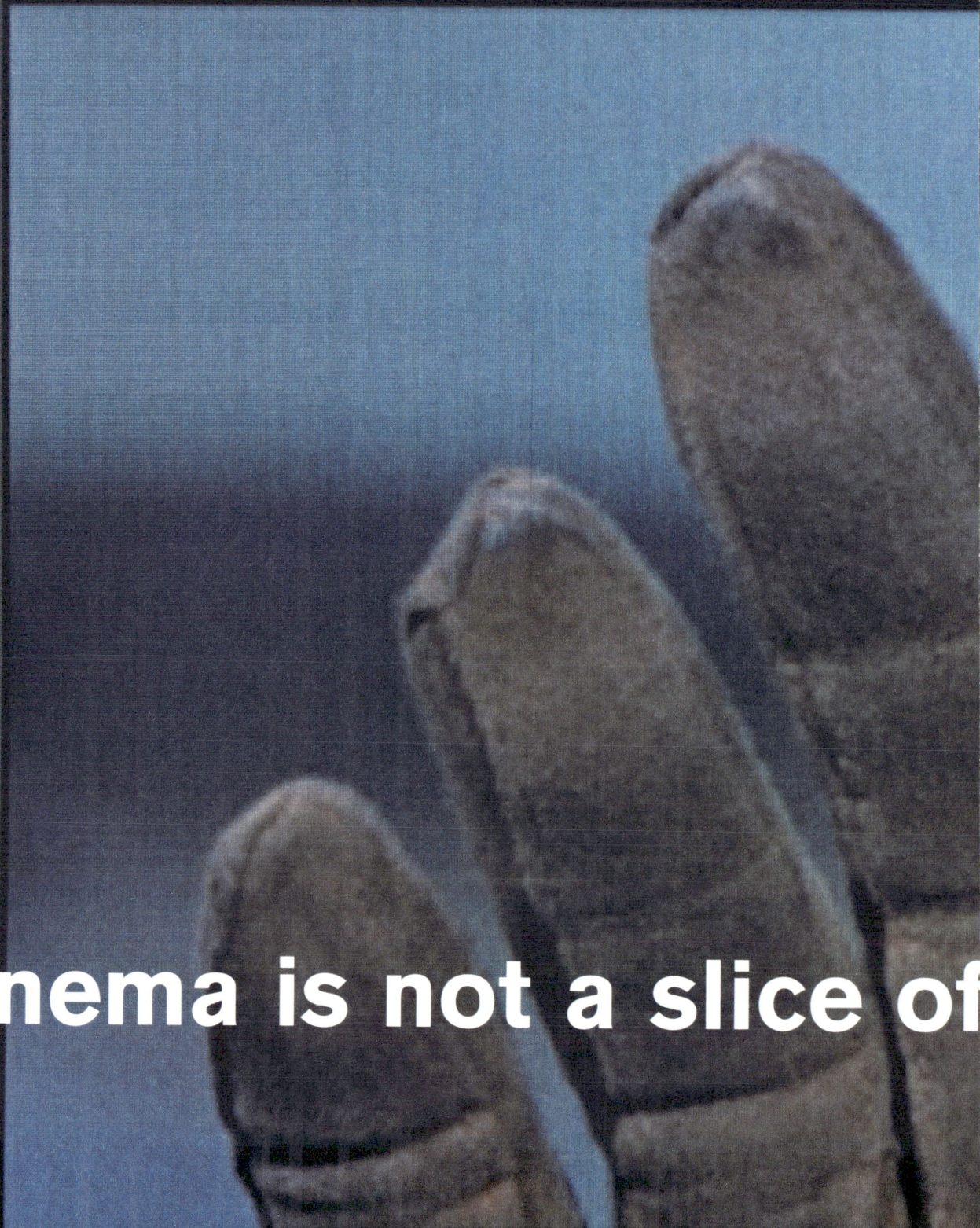

Cinema is not a slice of

00:24:32:20

ife, it's a piece of cake.

Alfred Hitchcock

Tiny bodies littered 5th Avenue. Hundreds of migrating birds... crashed into the Empire State Building early yesterday morning and plummeted to the street

'The New York Times', September 12, 1948

The birds, inadvertent suicides, hurled themselves at top speed into windows… Some died instantly. Some survived the long drop to the pavement… Not only was the intermittent plob of the birds disturbing… but particularly weird was the shrill chirping of many injured birds that dropped…

'Sept. 11, 1948: Winking Through History' by Eric Roston

Looking for Alfred

The Hitchcock Castings

New York

April 12 / 13, 2004
Deitch Projects
26 Wooster Street

Caroline Sinclair Casting

Merwin Goldsmith, Hitchcock double

Hitchcock, being pulled away:

But I'm Alfred Hitchcock, I am, I can prove it!

Man in white:

Sure, sure, everybody is...

Alfred Hitchcock Presents, Episode #10: The Case of Mr. Pelham,
broadcast on December 4, 1955

PROPS :

+ RAIN & WIND MACHINE

- BOWLER
- UMBRELLAS
- SUITS
- MOBILES

 VENDING MACHINE

+ KID'S AIRPLANE MACHINE

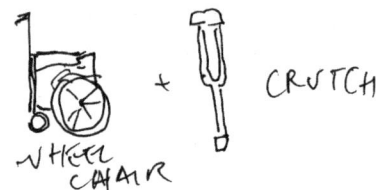 WHEEL CHAIR + CRUTCH

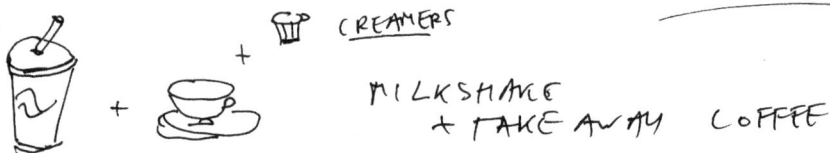 CREAMERS

MILKSHAKE + TAKE AWAY COFFEE

 SODA CANE + HOT DOG

 CIGARS + CARDS

 ? CLOCK

? BANDAGE AIDS ⊕

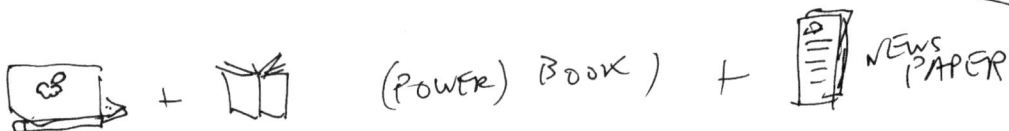 BUS + CAR TAXI ?

 + (POWER) BOOK) + NEWS PAPER

 KLEENEX

+ TREE LEAVES X 10.00

 BIRDCAGE + eggs

 CLEANING CART CLEANING STUFF

 WET FLOOR

 PICNIC BAG (BANANA) + THERMOS

ANIMALS

 BALLOONS

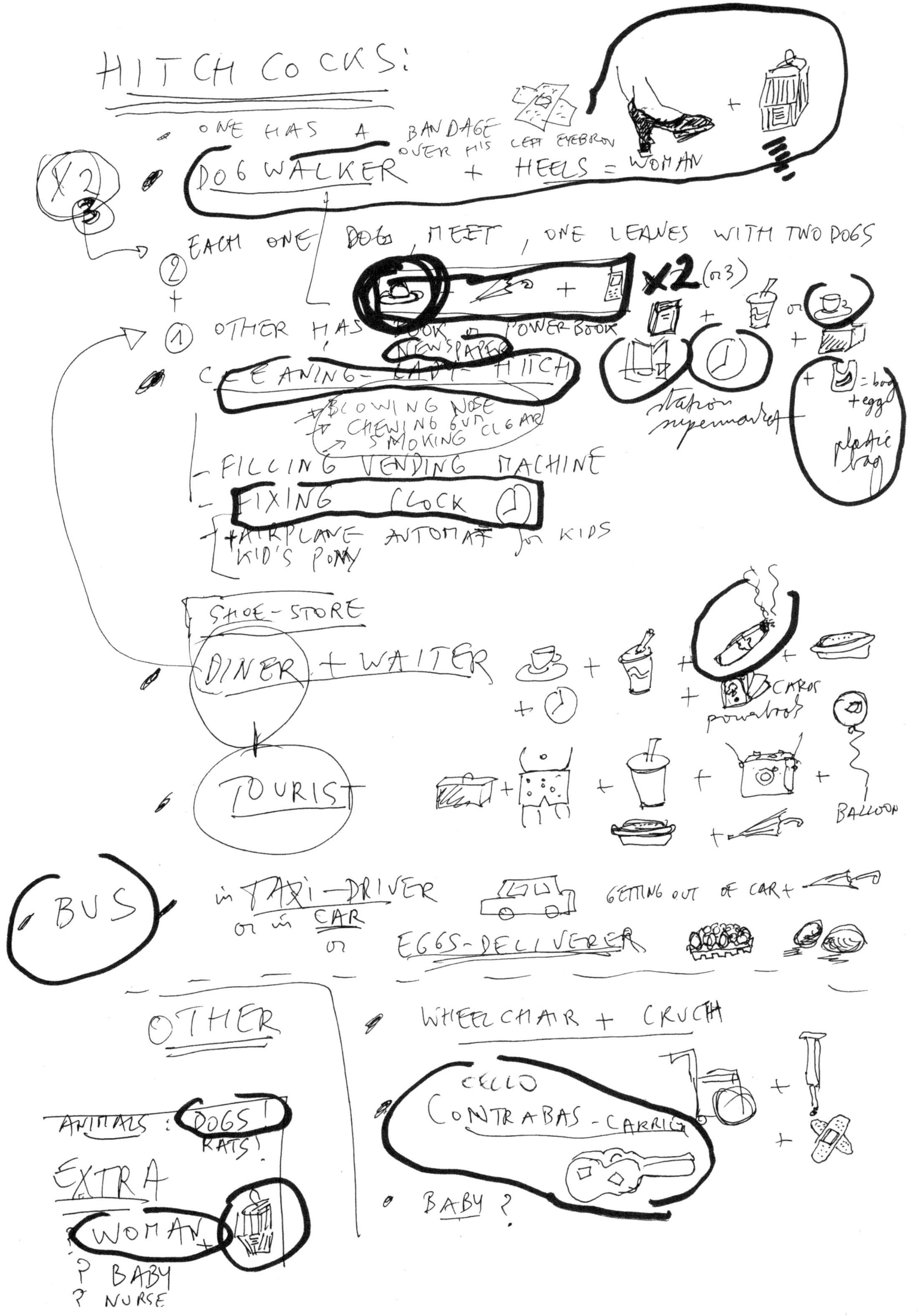

HITCH COCKS:

○ ONE HAS A BANDAGE OVER HIS LEFT EYEBROW

Ⓧ2 ● DOG WALKER   + HEELS = WOMAN

③

② EACH ONE DOG MEET , ONE LEAVES WITH TWO DOGS

① OTHER HAS BOOK or POWER BOOK   ×2 (or 3)
        NEWSPAPER

● CLEANING - LADY - HITCH
        → BLOWING NOSE
        → CHEWING GUM
           SMOKING CIGAR

- FILLING VENDING MACHINE
- FIXING CLOCK
- AIRPLANE AUTOMAT for KIDS
  KID'S PONY

SHOE - STORE

DINER + WAITER

5 TOURIST

CAROS
powateos

BALLOON

BUS   in TAXI - DRIVER   GETTING OUT OF CAR +
       or in CAR
             or EGGS - DELIVERER

OTHER   ● WHEELCHAIR + CRUTCH

                CELLO
           ● CONTRABAS - CARRIER

ANIMALS : DOGS!
           RATS!

EXTRA
? WOMAN +   ● BABY ?
? BABY
? NURSE

station
supermarket

= bag
+ egg
plastic
bag

Television is like the American Toaster, you push the button and the same thing pops up everytime.

Alfred Hitchcock

Kevin Carolan, Hitchcock double

Scene   Shot   Location

Scene	Shot	Location
⑥	⑥	arcade (p.o.v. stairs)

Cast required

1. hitch ③ (RON)
2. ....
3. ....
4. ....

— RON JUST TURNED TOWARDS TIPPI
— OTHER H— AROUND?
+ OTHER HATS BLOWN OFF TOO?

Art direction and props

— HAT + NYLON TREAD TO PULL HAT OFF HEAD
— WIND MACHINE
— LEAVES   raven flies up as well !
— raven

Shot description

① HITCH 3 LOOSES HIS HAT IN THE WIND. HIS HAIR FLUTTERS UP. AND LEAVES FLY INTO VIEW.

e.g. HITCH 3 's FACE (RON) IS FULLY REVEALED IN PROFILE.

quite close to stairs!

② RAVEN FLIES UP OR SOUND ONLY

SCREECH!

SH

SSS

Camera

1. STAY ON HITCH 3 FACE
2. FOLLOW HAT UP TO THE FLOOR

Lighting ....

HAT DROPS AS RAVEN FLIES UP OR AT LEAST NOISE

bird

hat rolls direction royal suite from stairs !!

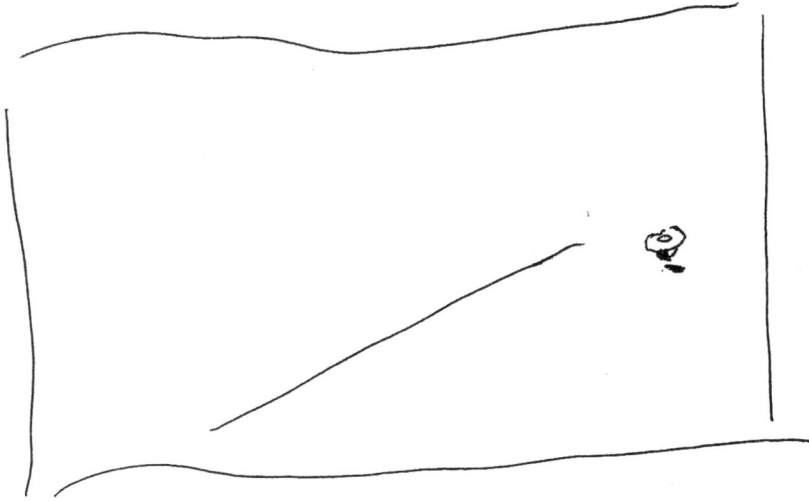

Alfred Hitchcock on the psychiatrist's sofa

Then I dreamed I was in a huge theatre where one of my motion pictures was being shown. But the theatre was absolutely empty, not a full seat anywhere. On one wall was a gigantic mirror, and when I looked into it, I didn't see my own face…

Alfred Hitchcock Presents, Episode # 69: The Three Dreams of Mr. Findlater, broadcast on April 21, 1957

Merwin Goldsmith, Hitchcock double

Matt Hyland, Hitchcock double

Jonathan Williams
Hitchcock double

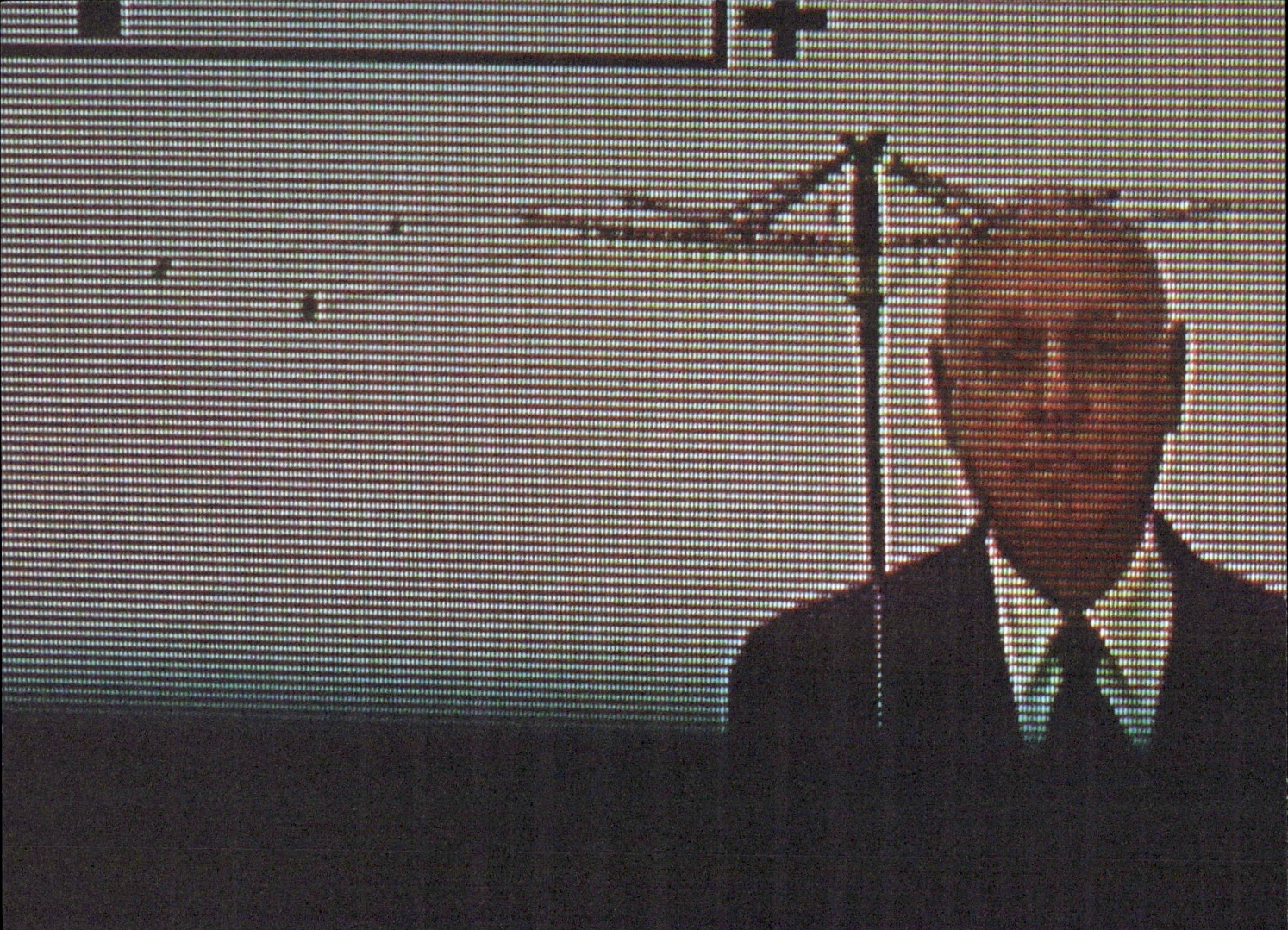

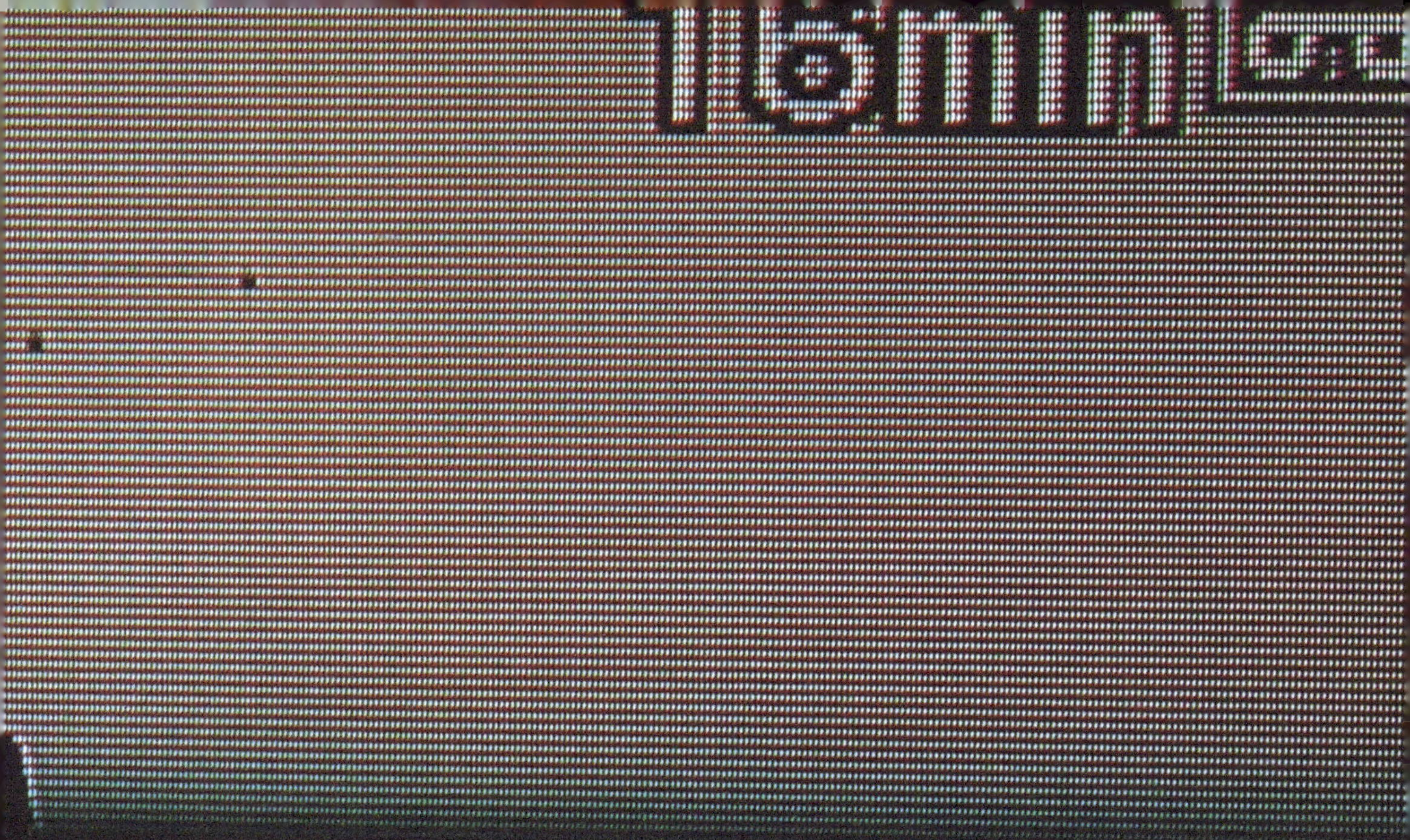

From: Hisami Kuroiwa
To: Daragh Reeves
Cc: Johan Grimonprez
Date: Thursday, April 8, 2004 11:24 AM
Subject: props

Hi Daragh and Johan:
For your info:
'Wool Bowlers' hat can be purchased at Arnold Hatters (212)768-3781,
535 8th avenue, 36-37th street, 4 sizes available, from $40 up to purchase
one. My number is (212) --- ----, and mobile is (917) --- ----

Thanks, Hisami

Scene   Shot   Location

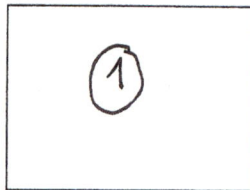

Scene	Shot	Location
③	①	coatrack room arcade

Cast required

1. .... raven?
2. ....
3. ....
4.
   (cello)

Art direction and props   coat + umbrella ....
....
.... coatrack ....
.... light bulb swings ....
.... raven

Shot description   static shot of umbrella slightly
... moving hanging together with coat on
... coatrack. Raven perched on the coatrack nearby.
....
....

Camera   ... static ....

Lighting   ...? lightbulb swings and cast shadows

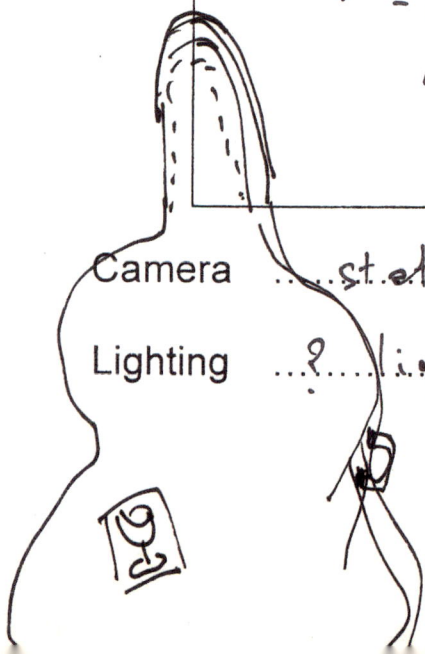

SCRATCH
SCRATCH

Jonathan Williams, Hitchcock double

egy ⟶ Pd BA

Aeps comito

PSK ②

n° # (15)

C.V.
DOG
BARKING

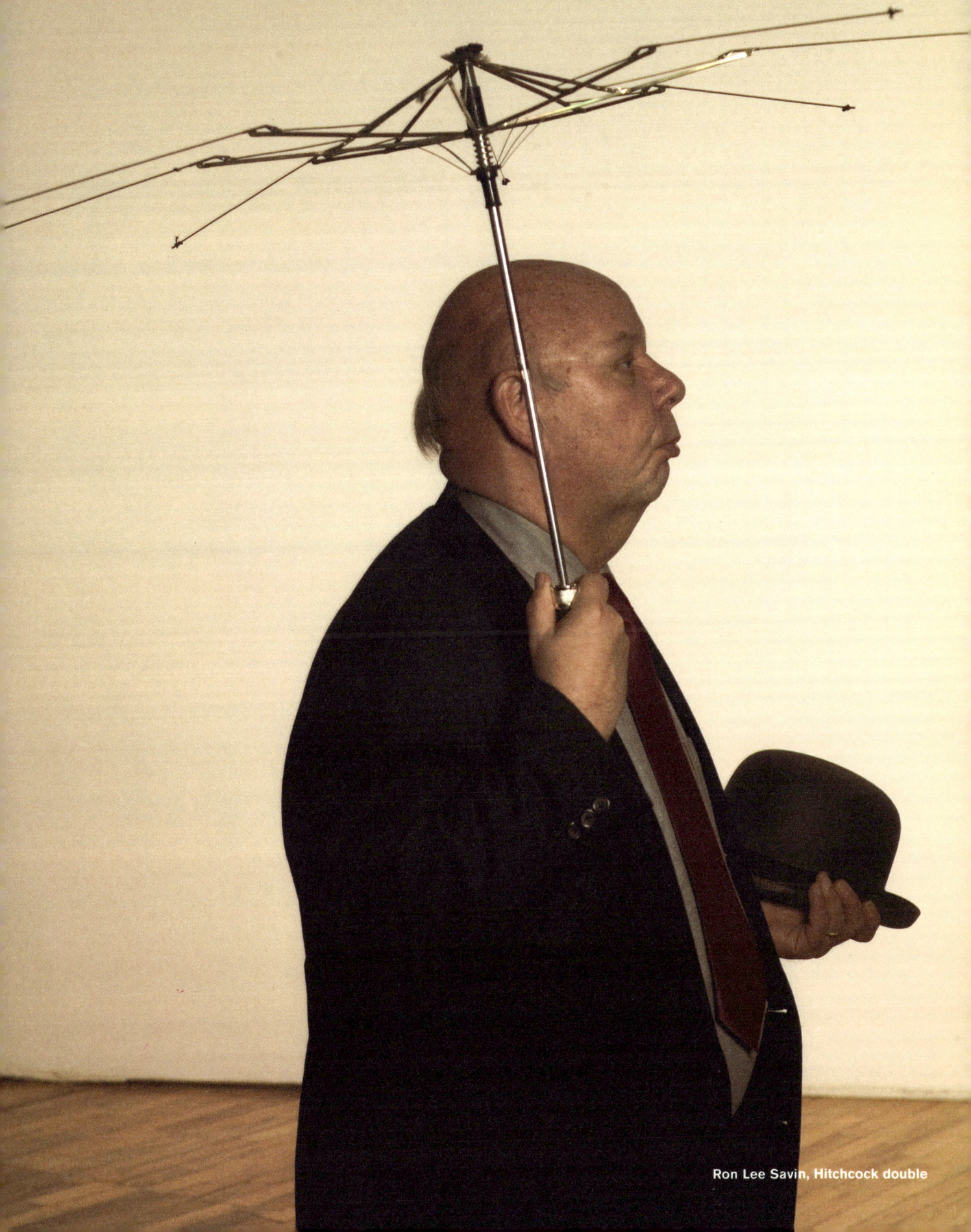

Ron Lee Savin, Hitchcock double

I never eat leg of lamb without thinking of the 'ticking lamb', the most perfect murder weapon of my entire career. It goes like this: actress Barbara Bel Geddes learns from her unsympathetic husband of many years that he is leaving her. She kills him with a frozen leg of lamb. Then she cooks that leg of lamb while policemen are searching for the murder weapon, and she serves them the delicious leg of lamb.

Alfred Hitchcock in Charlotte Chandler, 'It's only a Movie', Simon & Schuster, New York, 2005

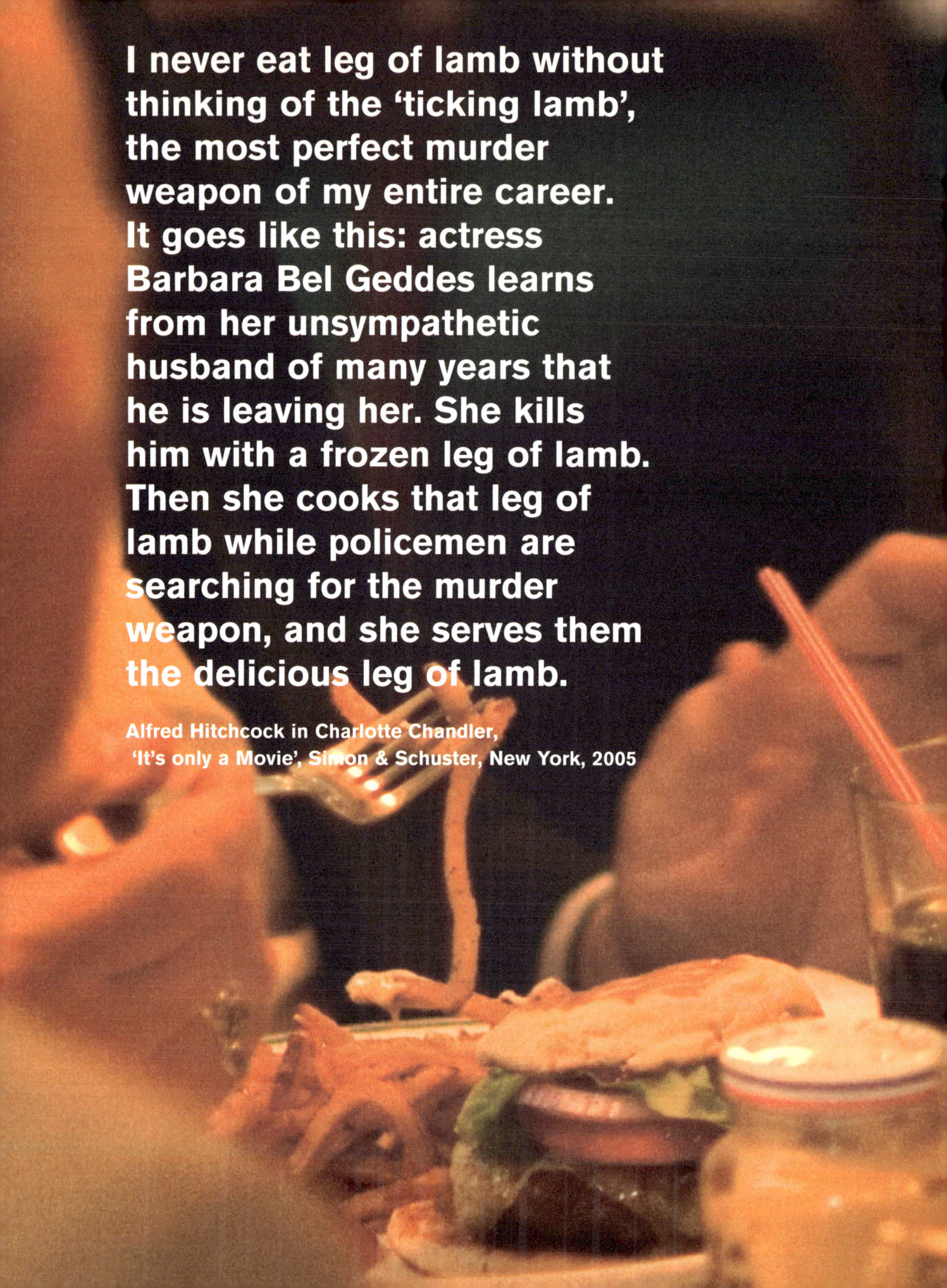

Hitchcock dinner, Lucky Strike Café, New York casting, 2004

Casting Around: Hitchcock's Absence

Thomas Elsaesser

Alfred Hitchcock #1:

I'm not Hitchcock.

Alfred Hitchcock Presents, Episode #49: Jonathan, broadcast on December 2, 1956

Casting Around: Hitchcock's Absence

Thomas Elsaesser

But in his Absence he still Commands the Scene

In January 2001, just after his death had been announced, I noticed, on the back of the Dutch film magazine 'Skrien's Christmas number, a photo by Johan van der Keuken, renowned Amsterdam documentarist. It showed a bend in a single-lane tarmac road, cut into rocks like a wedge, on a fairly steep incline. A holiday snap, taken in Southern Spain, where an ailing van der Keuken had fled to escape the inclement weather at home. What arrested my eye was the caption he gave it: 'The spirit of Hitchcock has just passed and disappeared around the corner. But in his absence he still commands the scene.'[1] It struck me as a surprisingly resonant, if unexpected juxtaposition, turning a banal shot into a moment of mysterious menace, reminiscent of no less than three Cary Grant 'dangerous driving' scenes: in *Suspicion*, *To Catch a Thief* and *North by Northwest*. Perhaps after all an apt homage to the master of montage and innuendo, from another master of montage and innuendo, however far apart the two filmmakers were in every other respect. I gave it no further thought, more preoccupied with the loss of a director whom his own country had never given his due. Over the years, however, as I noticed how inescapable and indispensable references to Hitchcock had become in my field, and not only in academic film studies, but for artists, curators, photographers, filmmakers, biographers, and critics, I began to wonder why 'in his absence, he still commands the scene'. Indeed: why twenty-five years after his death, his absence has become such a presence.

A brief reminder of just how ubiquitous, but also how elusive he is: type 'Alfred Hitchcock' into Amazon.com 'books' and you have more than 7,000 hits. Even subtracting the scores of ghosted Ellery Queen mystery paperbacks that appear under his name, there are well over 600 books in print that deal with his films, his life, his women, his stars, his collaborators and associates. Look under DVDs, and all his films (as well as many of the TV shows) are available in digitally remastered re-issues, bundled collections, special editions and boxed sets.[2] If this is the thick ground-cover of his fame, academia and the art world provide the taller trees. Eric Rohmer and Claude Chabrol's study from 1957, Robin Wood's 'Hitchcock's Films' from 1965, Truffaut's interview book 'Le Cinema selon Hitchcock' from 1966 (eng. tr. 1967) and Jean Douchet's 'Alfred Hitchcock' (1967) set the stage. But instead of four books in ten years, the average since the 1980s has been more than tenfold that number for each decade. The 1980s and 1990s

1 The photo is online at http://esvc001069.wic023u.server-web.com/5/elsaesser.html

2 'Hitchcock is already everywhere in American culture – in video stores and on cable TV, in film courses and in a stream of critical studies and biographies that shows no sign of letting up, in remakes and re-workings and allusions that mine the oeuvre as a kind of folklore.' (Geoffrey O'Brien, 'Hitchcock: The Hidden Power', 'New York Review of Books' vol. 48, no. 18, November 15, 2001)

saw artists bring Hitchcock to the gallery: Judith Barry (1980), Victor Burgin (1984), Cindy Sherman (1986), Stan Douglas (1989), Christian Marclay (1990), Douglas Gordon (1993), David Reed (1994), Pierre Huyghe (1995), Tony Oursler (1996), Cindy Bernard (1997), Christoph Girardet and Matthias Müller (1999).[3]

Filmmakers, almost too numerous to count, have rendered homage to Hitchcock's films: foremost, Brian de Palma who, starting with *Obsession* (1976), *Dressed to Kill* (1980) and *Blow-Out* (1981), has virtually devoted his career to *Vertigo* remakes. David Mamet's *The Spanish Prisoner* (1997), Robert Zemeckis' *What Lies Beneath* (2000), Steven Spielberg's *Munich* (2005; the phone bomb scene) have all been praised for their 'Hitchcockian moments', while every film version of Patricia Highsmith's Ripley novels, from *Plein Soleil* (1960) to *The American Friend* (1977) and from *The Talented Mr Ripley* (1999) to *Ripley's Game* (2002) has had to pass the Hitchcock (*Strangers on a Train*) litmus test. Roman Polanski might well be considered the most gifted among Hitchcock disciples: much of his oeuvre is a careful, as well as witty response to the challenge that Hitchcock presents: *Repulsion* his *Marnie*, *Frantic* his *North by Northwest*, *The Tenant* his *Psycho* and *Bitter Moon* his *Vertigo*. Gus van Sant famously restaged *Psycho* shot-for-shot in 1998,[4] and most recently, the Shanghai filmmaker Ye Lou has been introduced to Western audiences as 'Hitchcock with a Chinese Face'.[5]

To each his or her own: academics have praised Hitchcock for defending family values[6] but also for sadistically intertwining love, lust and death.[7] He has been compared to Shakespeare and Mozart, and 'outed' as an eternal Catholic schoolboy racked with guilt. Writers have identified a misogynist Hitchcock and a feminist Hitchcock,[8] an Oedipal Hitchcock,[9] a homophobe Hitchcock and a 'queer' Hitchcock.[10] There is the cold-war anti-communist Hitchcock of *Topaz* and *Torn Curtain*, and the hot-war anti-fascist Hitchcock not only of *Saboteur*, *Foreign Correspondent* and *Notorious*,[11] but also present in *Shadow of a Doubt*. He has made fun of psychoanalysis in *Rear Window* and *Psycho*, but he is Jacques Lacan's best interpreter.[12] There is a Gothic-Romantic, a Victorian,[13] an Edwardian Hitchcock, with his imagination steeped in E.Λ. Poe and French decadence,[14] and a Modernist Hitchcock,[15] influenced in turn by Weimar Expressionism,[16] French Surrealism and Russian montage constructivism. And, of course, there is the postmodern Hitchcock, already deconstructing his own presuppositions in *Vertigo* or *Family Plot*.[17] The 'British Hitchcock' has been given new cultural contours and local history roots, to balance the general preference for his American period.[18] And in recent years, we have had Hitchcock the Philosopher:[19] but which philosopher? There is a Schopenhauerian Hitchcock,[20] a Heideggerian Hitchcock and a Derridean Hitchcock, several Deleuzian Hitchcocks, a stab at a Nietzschean Hitchcock (*Rope*, of course) and most recently, a Wittgensteinian Hitchcock.

3 Most of these artists were brought together in the group show 'Notorious: Alfred Hitchcock and Contemporary Art', a 1999 exhibition at the Museum of Modern Art, Oxford.

4 Constantine Santas, 'The Remake of Psycho (Gus Van Sant, 1998): Creativity or Cinematic Blasphemy?', 'Senses of Cinema' (Great Director series) and Slavoj Žižek, 'Is there a proper way to remake a Hitchcock film?', 'Lacanian Ink' (www.lacan.com / hitch.htm).

5 Jerome Silbergeld, 'Hitchcock with a Chinese Face: Cinematic Doubles, Oedipal Triangles, and China's Moral Voice', Seattle, University of Washington Press, (2004).

6 Lesley Brill, 'The Hitchcock Romance: Love and Irony in Hitchcock's Films', Princeton, N.J., Princeton University Press, (1988).

7 Love, lust and death are the words used for the Scottie-Madeleine relation in *Vertigo*, or to typify the attraction-repulsion between Mark and Marnie in *Marnie*. See Norman H. Holland on *Vertigo*, or Tony Lee Moral, 'Hitchcock and the Making of Marnie'. Manchester, Manchester University Press, (2003).

8 Sander H. Lee, 'Alfred Hitchcock: Misogynist or Feminist?' 'Post Script', vol. 10 no. 3. 1991 Summer, pp. 38–48.

9 David Kelly, 'Oedipus at Los Angeles: Hitch and the Tragic Muse', 'Senses of Cinema', 24:2003 Jan–Feb.

10 Tania Modleski, 'The Women who Knew Too Much: Hitchcock and Feminist Theory'. New York: Routledge, (1988). Theodore Price, 'Hitchcock and Homosexuality: his 50-year Obsession with Jack the Ripper and the Superbitch Prostitute: A Psychoanalytic View'. Metuchen, N.J.: Scarecrow Press, (1992). Robert J. Corber, 'In the Name of National Security: Hitchcock, Homophobia, and the Political Construction of Gender in Postwar America'. Duke University Press, (1993); MJ Robinson, 'The Poetics of Camp in the Films of Alfred Hitchcock', 'Rocky Mountain Review' vol. 51, no. 1, Spring 2000.

Alfred Hitchcock #2:

Alfred will play my part.

Alfred Hitchcock Presents, Episode #49: Jonathan,
broadcast on December 2, 1956

How can a man – and his work – be so many apparently contradictory things to so many different people? What is it that draws them – and us – to Hitchcock and makes him return, time and again, as so many doubles of his own improbable self? Proliferating even as they voice their protest, each one implicitly claims the kind of authenticity which must strip the others of their usurped pretentions. Slavoj Žižek, himself not someone to pass up an opportunity to bring Hitchcock into the debate, irrespective of the subject, once suggested a plausible if possibly tautologous answer: his claim is that Hitchcock has since his death in 1980 increasingly functioned not as an object of study or analysis, but as a mirror to film studies, in its shifting contemporary obsessions and insecurities. Commenting, by self-referentially double-backing on his own contributions to the unabatedly thriving Hitchcock industry, he diagnoses the logic behind the various hermeneutic moves and changes in reputation and predilection I have just enumerated, as the effects of transference (a major theme, of course, in Hitchcock's work, itself magisterially dissected in the very first book of the cycle, the Rohmer/Chabrol study). This transference has made of Hitchcock himself a monstrous figure, at once too close and too far, a (maternal) superego 'blur' as much as a super-male Godlike 'subject supposed to know'.[21]

According to this logic, Hitchcock occupies the place not so much of the film-auteur analysed, as of the (psycho-) analyst, analysing: listening impassively to the interpretative talking (auto-) cure, his famous silhouette over the years getting to look more and more like those giant faces of the Egyptian goddess in the British Museum in *Blackmail*, the Statue of Liberty (in *Saboteur*) and the Mount Rushmore Presidents (in *North By Northwest*). 'Hitchcock' is always already there: in place and in control, when the interpreting critic arrives with yet another definitive or diabolically ingenious reading. The various stages of Hitchcock's reception from the late 1950s to the 1990s and beyond, thus do not even chart the inner dynamic of film studies, as scholars refine, redefine or overturn the reigning critical paradigms. What drives the Hitchcock hermeneutic (wind-) mills would be an impulse altogether more philosophically serious, namely the desire to overcome, across transference and mirror doubling (and thus doomed to fail), the deadlocks of ontological groundlessness: from 'pure cinema' to 'pure deconstruction', as it were, – and beyond.[22]

What is plausible in this thesis is that Hitchcock, once canonised as the towering figure of his art – no different indeed from Shakespeare, Mozart, Jane Austen or James Joyce – feeds an academic industry that, once set up and institutionally secure, largely sustains itself without further input from the 'real world' other than reflecting the changing intellectual fashions of the respective disciplines. The author and the work become a sort of 'black box' into which

11 Sam P. Simone, 'Hitchcock As Activist: Politics and the War Films'. Ann Arbor, Mich.: UMI Research Press, c. 1985.

12 Robert Samuels, 'Hitchcock's bi-textuality: Lacan, Feminisms, and Queer Theory'. Albany: State University of New York Press, (1998).

13 Paula Marantz Cohen, 'Alfred Hitchcock: The Legacy of Victorianism'. Lexington: University Press of Kentucky, (1995).

14 Dennis R. Perry, 'Bibliography of Scholarship Linking Alfred Hitchcock and Edgar Allan Poe.' 'Hitchcock Annual' [2000–2001], pp. 163–73.

15 Peter J. Hutchings, 'Modernity: a film by Alfred Hitchcock'. 'Senses of Cinema' Issue No. 6, May 2000.

16 Sidney Gottlieb, 'Early Hitchcock: The German Influence', 'Hitchcock Annual' [1999–2000], pp. 100–130.

17 Richard Allen, 'Hitchcock, or the pleasures of meta-skepticism', 'October' no. 89 (Summer 1999), pp. 69–86.

18 Charles Barr, 'English Hitchcock'. Moffat: Cameron & Hollis, (1999).

19 Robert J. Yanal, 'Hitchcock as philosopher', Jefferson, N.C.: McFarland & Co., 2005.

20 Ken Mogg, 'The Alfred Hitchcock Story'. Titan Books, London, (1999) most persistently and quite persuasively argues for Hitchcock as a disciple of Schopenhauer's 'World as Will and Representation'.

21 'Hitchcock as the theoretical phenomenon that we have witnessed in recent decades – the endless flow of books, articles, university courses, conference panels – is a postmodern phenomenon par excellence. It relies on the extraordinary transference his work sets in motion: [his] elevation into a God-like demiurge […] is simply the transferential relationship where Hitchcock functions as the 'subject supposed to know'.' 'Introduction: Alfred Hitchcock, or, the Form and Its Historical Mediation,' in Slavoj Žižek (ed.), 'Everything You always Wanted to Know About Lacan: (But were Afraid to Ask Hitchcock)', London, New York, Verso, (1992), p. 10.

22 For Hitchcock, Derrida and deconstruction, see: Christopher Morris, 'The Hanging Figure: On Suspense and the Films of Alfred Hitchcock' (Westport, CT: Greenwood Press, 2002).

23 See also John Belton, 'Can Hitchcock Be Saved from Hitchcock Studies?', 'Cineaste', 28:4 [Fall 2003], pp. 16–22.

24 Robert E. Kapsis, 'Hitchcock: The Making of a Reputation', Chicago: University of Chicago Press, (1992).

25 'Salvador Dalí was unique with his representation of dripping clocks. Picasso was unique with his two-eyed profiles, and Van Gogh was known for his swirling brush strokes in *Starry Night*. And there's a reason why people stare intently at these art works in the galleries rather than the vinyl placemats and canvas diaper bags resembling them in the museum gift shops. Although replicas can be just as appealing to the eye, without the innovation the masterpiece demanded in its conception, a replica can never compare to its original. That's why I still, to this day, have not seen the 1990s remake of *Psycho*, and that's why I'd like to throw rotten tomatoes at every *Mr. and Mrs. Smith* movie poster I see.' Elisha Sauers, 'Hitch-what-ian?', 'Indiana Daily Student', June 16, 2005.

26 David M. Lubin, '"Hitchcock and Art: Fatal Coincidences', Centre Georges Pompidou, Paris', 'Art Forum', Nov, 2001.

everything can be put and from which anything can be pulled.[23] What is close to a tautology, however, is that in thus turning the fascination and 'return' back to the writers and academics, it creates a closed loop. But why such a loop should form in the first place, around this particular figure and director, rather than another, and why the magic seems to work not just for academics, but extends well beyond to popular audiences, artists, novelists, the general public, is less plausibly explained, because it is already presupposed.

FROM A WORK TO A WORLD

If we grant that Hitchcock, that constant reference point, now almost synonymous with the cinema itself, has become indispensable in the wider field of art, culture and the popular imagination, then something must have happened, both to his work and to the cinema, which he personifies and embodies. To recapitulate: from being a gifted craftsman behind the camera, technically skilled and ambitious, with a morbid imagination covered up by a mordant wit (the view of the British establishment well into the 1960s) and of being a superb showman with a rare talent for second-guessing popular taste and an uncanny gift for self-promotion (the Hollywood view, almost up to his death in 1980),[24] Hitchcock, some time between the 1970s and 2000, also became one of the great artists of the 20th century, not just without peers in his own profession, but on a par with Picasso, Duchamp, Proust and Kafka.[25] Like Kafka, his name has become an adjective, and like Picasso, everyone knows not only what his work looks like, but what it 'feels' like, whether they have studied it or not. These artists define more than an age, an art-form or a sensibility; they are a way of seeing the world and even of being in the world.

Hitchcock's consecration became complete and official in 2001, when first in Montreal and then at the Centre Pompidou in Paris 'Hitchcock et l'Art: Coincidences Fatales' opened to wide acclaim and largely rave reviews. Curated by Dominique Paini and Guy Cogeval, the exhibition was a fetishist's paradise: accompanied by the strains of Bernard Herrmann's music, the visitor entered via a large room where 'pinpoint spotlights stabbed out of the darkness at twenty-one small display cases mounted on a grid of twenty-one black columns. Each glass case bore a single cherished object arranged on a bed of red satin: the gleaming scissors from *Dial M for Murder*, the bread knife from *Blackmail*, the key from *Notorious*, the cigarette lighter from *Strangers on a Train*, the black brassiere from *Psycho*.'[26]

This distillation (and dilation) of the films to the telling detail, to the tactile object, the dizzying erotic power emanating from these strangely familiar and murderously innocent objects, like deadly insects or poisonous snakes

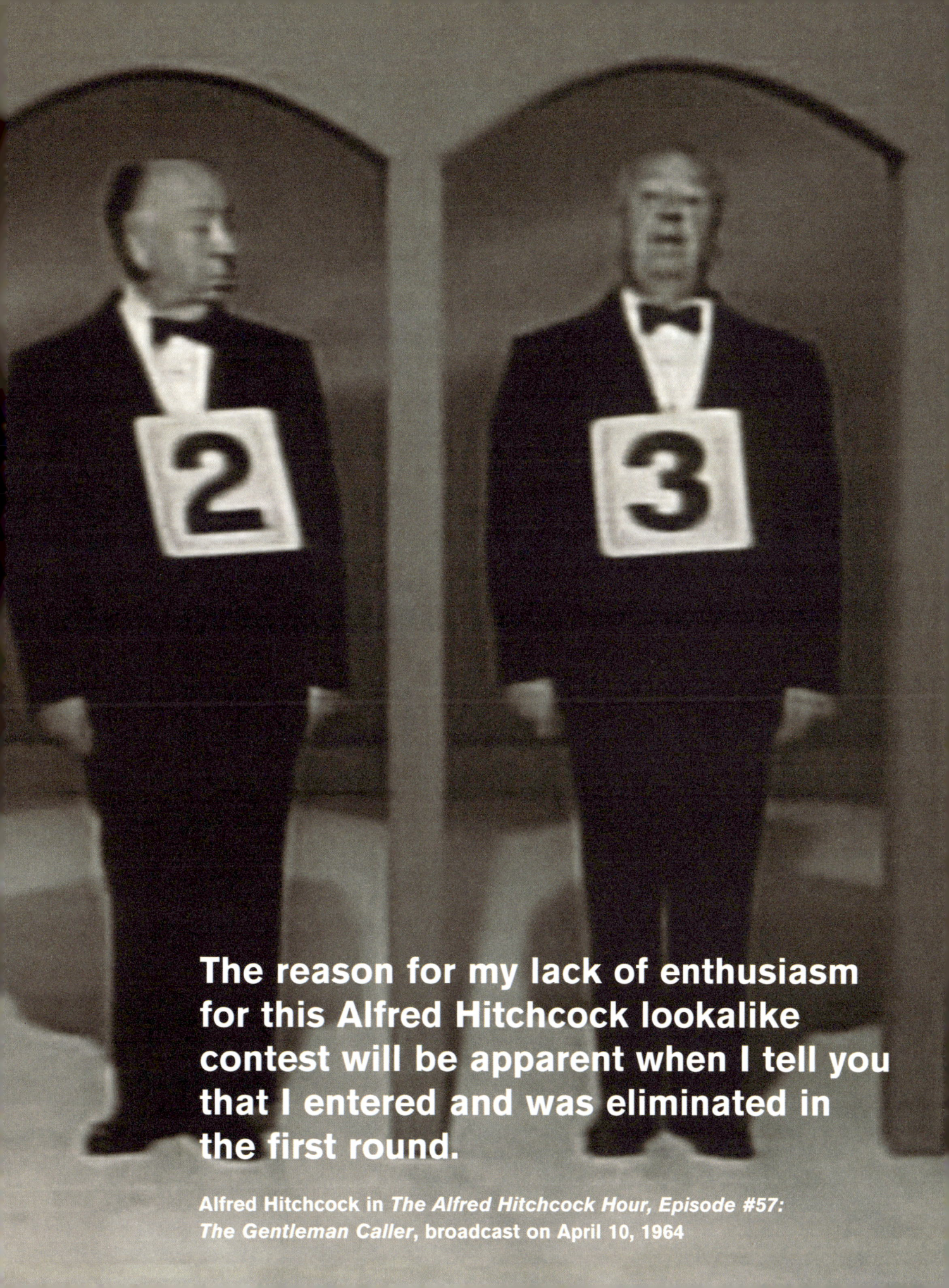

The reason for my lack of enthusiasm for this Alfred Hitchcock lookalike contest will be apparent when I tell you that I entered and was eliminated in the first round.

Alfred Hitchcock in *The Alfred Hitchcock Hour, Episode #57: The Gentleman Caller*, broadcast on April 10, 1964

under glass, also seemed to be endorsed by the citation from Jean Luc Godard, hung over the entrance portal as majestically and incontrovertibly as the words inscribed in Dante's Hell:

> People forget why Joan Fontaine was leaning over the cliff [...], why Janet Leigh stops at the Bates Motel, and why Teresa Wright remains in love with Uncle Charlie. They forget what Henry Fonda was not altogether guilty of, and why exactly the American government employed the services of Ingrid Bergman. But they remember a car in the desert. They remember a glass of milk, the vanes of a windmill, a hairbrush. They remember a wine rack, a pair of glasses, a fragment of music, a set of keys. Because through them and with them, Alfred Hitchcock succeeded where Alexander the Great, Julius Caesar, Napoleon, and Hitler failed: in taking control of the universe. Perhaps ten thousand people have not forgotten Cézanne's apples, but a billion spectators will recall the cigarette lighter in *Strangers on a Train*, and if Alfred Hitchcock has been the only poète maudit to achieve success, it is because he was the greatest creator of forms of the twentieth century and that it is forms which tell us, finally, what there is at the bottom of things; and what is art except that by which forms become style.[27]

The passage (originally from *Histoire(s) du cinéma*) is justly famous, full of the extravagant hyperbole of the youthful Godard, but now intoned with the growl and rumble of late Godard, blackened by the ashes of the Holocaust, which he sees himself as having survived, but which has cost the cinema its soul. Godard makes the all-important move from Hitchcock the kinky fetishist to Hitchcock the canny world-conqueror. Without the hyperbole and the apocalypse, one can say that the 'Hitchcock' posthumously anointed at the Pompidou,[28] is now no longer an artist among other artists, with a body of work and an inimitable stylistic signature, however unique this is for a British commercial filmmaker working within the Hollywood studio-system, but that he is a 'world': complete, self-sufficient, not just immediately recognisable in and by its details, but consistent through and through: in short, holding the promise or the premonition that his cinema and thus *the cinema* can be/has become an ontology, an inventory of what is and can exist.

At any rate, it seems a battle is on, about the reality status of each: the world of Hitchcock/Hollywood and the world of history/memory, and it is not always certain which will win. Perhaps this very battle is what we need to witness, because it is as much an ontological one as it is perceptual. Ontological:

27 Jean Luc Godard, 'Histoire(s) du Cinéma' vol 4, Paris, Gallimard, (1998), quoted also in Geoffrey O'Brien, loc. cit.

28 James M. Vest, 'Hitchcock and France: the forging of an auteur', Westport, Conn., Praeger, (2003).

29 In David Mitchell's novel 'Cloud Atlas', there is a scene where one of the main protagonists, Luisa Rey reports an interview she did with Hitchcock, in which she 'put it to the great man, the key to fictitious terror is partition or containment: so long as the Bates Motel is sealed off from our world, we want to peer in, like at a scorpion enclosure.' Cited by A.S. Byatt, 'Overlapping Lives', 'The Guardian', March 6, 2004.

30 From Johan Grimonprez's interview-statement: 'What actually fascinated me in this new work, is how much our understanding of reality today is filtered through Hollywood imagery. For instance, when Hitchcock scholar Slavoj Žižek compared the 9/11 attack on the World Trade Centre to a real-life version of *The Birds*, he called it the ultimate Hitchcockian threat that suddenly appeared out of nowhere. He referred specifically to the scene when Melanie, played by Tippi Hedren, approaches the Bodega Bay pier in a small boat, and a single seagull, first perceived as an indistinguishable dark blot, unexpectedly swoops down and gashes her forehead. It is strikingly similar to the plane hitting the second World Trade Centre tower. In this sense 9/11 brought fiction back to haunt us as reality.'

31 Raymond Bellour, 'Les Oiseaux: Analyse d'une Séquence', in 'L'Analyse du Film', Paris, Albatros, (1979), [orig.: 'Cahiers du cinema' 216, 1969, pp. 24–38.]

32 'The collapse between what is real and what is fake is very much part of the exploration throughout *Looking for Alfred*, in particular with reference to lookalike culture. Film stars become fake imitations of their celebrity projections and in turn lookalikes, while adopting the attitudes of their cherished idol, become a more real version of what they try to look alike.' Interview with Johan Grimonprez.

the power of the cinema to define our reality, or as Jean Luc Nancy once put it: coming to terms with the possibility that 'the lie of the image is the truth of our world.' And perceptual: the philosophical stakes of mimesis, representation and simulation.[29] I come back to Johan van der Keuken. It is not only that 'in his absence he still commands the scene'. The scene only exists, because it reminds van der Keuken of Hitchcock. Has it come to the point, where we notice something, only because it repeats a scene from a movie? In *Sans Soleil*, Chris Marker, on a visit to San Francisco, can only see the Golden Gate Bridge as an artefact from Hitchcock's *Vertigo*, a gesture repeated by Cindy Bernard, when she took her photograph *Ask the Dust: Vertigo* (1958/1990) from the exact spot (now railed off) where Scottie fished Madeleine out of the water and carried her back to his car. For his television programme *The Pervert's Guide to the Cinema*, Slavoj Žižek went to Bodega Bay, took a boat, and played Melanie, in order to deliver once more the cage with the love birds and to re-experience the first attack of the gulls,[30] a scene from *The Birds* that had already served Raymond Bellour for one of the most dense and delirious pieces of close textual reading.[31] It became a sort of primal-scene of psychoanalytic film theory, next to the crop-dusting episode from *North By Northwest*, the Indiana Prairie Stop that many a Hitchcock fan (including myself) has tried to locate, and which Cindy Bernard again, claims to have found in her *Ask the Dust: North by Northwest* (1959/1990). Is Hitchcock's 'world' metonymically present, because these are the 'primal scenes' of an ontological switch, establishing a new 'order of things' an archive of first-cause references, of which the phenomenal world is merely the reflection and residue? Has his 'world' – and by extension, the world of (Hollywood) movies – become our Platonic Heaven, making its memory thus the 'hell' (of obsessions, fixations, murderous designs, palpitating terrors and feverish longings) which our 'returns' try to turn into a 'home', and to whose impossibly flawed endeavour our repetition compulsions bear witness? In other words, is one of the reasons we now have (Hitchcock) 'installations' in our museums due to the fact that these are the 'worlds' we need to, want to, but finally cannot install ourselves in?[32]

THE PARADOXES OF MIMESIS FROM PARRHASIOS TO HITCHCOCK

From a two-dimensional picture on the screen, Hitchcock's world invites one to think it three dimensional – to gratify an almost bodily urge to enter into it, to penetrate it, furnish it, surround oneself with it, irrespective of, or precisely because of one's awareness of the dangers, even courting them: besides repeating Norman Bates' gesture, it is the Scottie syndrome – taking *Vertigo* as the most accomplished version of the Hitchcockian *mal a voir*, the swooning sickness –

that sucks the viewer into his films, and of which *Psycho* would be the more hysterical spasm. It may explain why some artists have tried to 'inhabit' this universe by dilating it: Douglas Gordon's installation-projection *24 Hour Psycho*, by taking up a complete day, is wall-to-wall Hitchcock: not in space but in time. If such a move sounds drastic, the paradox it points to is nonetheless unavoidable: as Hitchcock never tired to point out, his films are all about artifice, not life-like realism,[33] so how can they exert such a strong mimetic pull? In other words, if after Hitchcock, Life Imitates the Movies, how did we get there, and especially how did Hitchcock get us there?

One obvious way that Hitchcock lures us in, Caligari-like conjuror and showman that he also was, is with his cameos, the walk-on parts which should now perhaps be described as 'walk-in' parts: not just in the sense that often enough, Hitchcock literally 'walks into' his own films, giving us, for a split-second, the double-take impression of seeing in 3-D. He also beckons us in, nowhere more so than in those cameos, where a quick look over the shoulder (most ag/trans/gressively in *Marnie*),[34] invites us to follow him along the corridors of his character's secret,[35] but initiating also a gesture of display, like a shopkeeper showing off his wares, or a gamekeeper presenting the habitats of exquisitely exotic, enigmatic or merely eccentric creatures. Hitchcock's films, at certain moments, become walk-in zoos, taking us on a safari of familiar, if far from open-range obsessions. At other times, scenes generate a pull of immersion, where one is led on, not by the master-magician himself, but by his female assistant, the blond heroine. She is the one who ventures into ominously silent attics, tries and rattles locked doors, or takes us down some dark passage way, no: down the cellar stairs in Norman Bates' house: an Alice, either falling into a Wonderland of screeching birds, or as in *Psycho*, of an equally screeching (if we're still listening), as well as grinning, mummy's skull.[36]

The 'walk-in' effect, as well as the beckoning gesture, invariably calls to mind the most famous of all stories of mimetic representation as a bodily effect, the story of the two Greek painters, Zeuxis and Parrhasios, as related by Pliny. Zeuxis once painted some grapes that were so realistic that birds swooped on the canvas and pecked at them. But then, his rival Parrhasios asked Zeuxis to his studio, keen to demonstrate a similar feat. Zeuxis, in front of the work, demanded Parrhasios to draw back the curtain, which hung across the canvas, in order to be able to judge for himself the skills of his colleague. But the curtain *was* the painting. Acknowledging that Parrhasios was the better of the two, Zeuxis said, 'I took in the birds, but you took me in.'

Besides the swooping birds, there is another point to this story that relates to Hitchcock. For whereas the life-like grapes give us versions of photo-realism,

[33] 'My movies are a piece of cake, not a slice of life' (Hitchcock). But see also Tom Cohen, 'Anti-mimesis From Plato to Hitchcock', Cambridge/New York, Cambridge University Press, (1994).

[34] This scene, too, has been exhaustively analysed by Raymond Bellour, 'Hitchcock the Enunciator', 'Camera Obscura' No. 2 Fall 1977, pp. 66–87.

[35] 'One crucial and recurring moment in the work is of Hitchcock meeting himself. The point where he turns his head and glances back refers to *Stage Fright* (1949) and *Marnie* (1964). I've mirrored these with the Hitchcock cameo from *Foreign Correspondent* (1940), where he passes someone on the street. This glancing back appears also recurrently in the casting sessions as we asked each impersonator to do this to camera.' Interview with Johan Grimonprez.

[36] 'He was in some sense our Lewis Carroll, populating his Wonderland with looking-glass inversions of the same world we inhabit: a world of spies and murderers, lovers and tennis players, actresses and jewel thieves. They exist, apparently, to make fascinating patterns in which the spectator, like the director before him, can become lost.' Geoffrey O'Brien, loc. cit.

After the break, Alfred and I shall return.

commercial

Alfred Hitchcock Presents, Episode #255: Ten O'Clock Tiger, broadcast on April 3, 1962

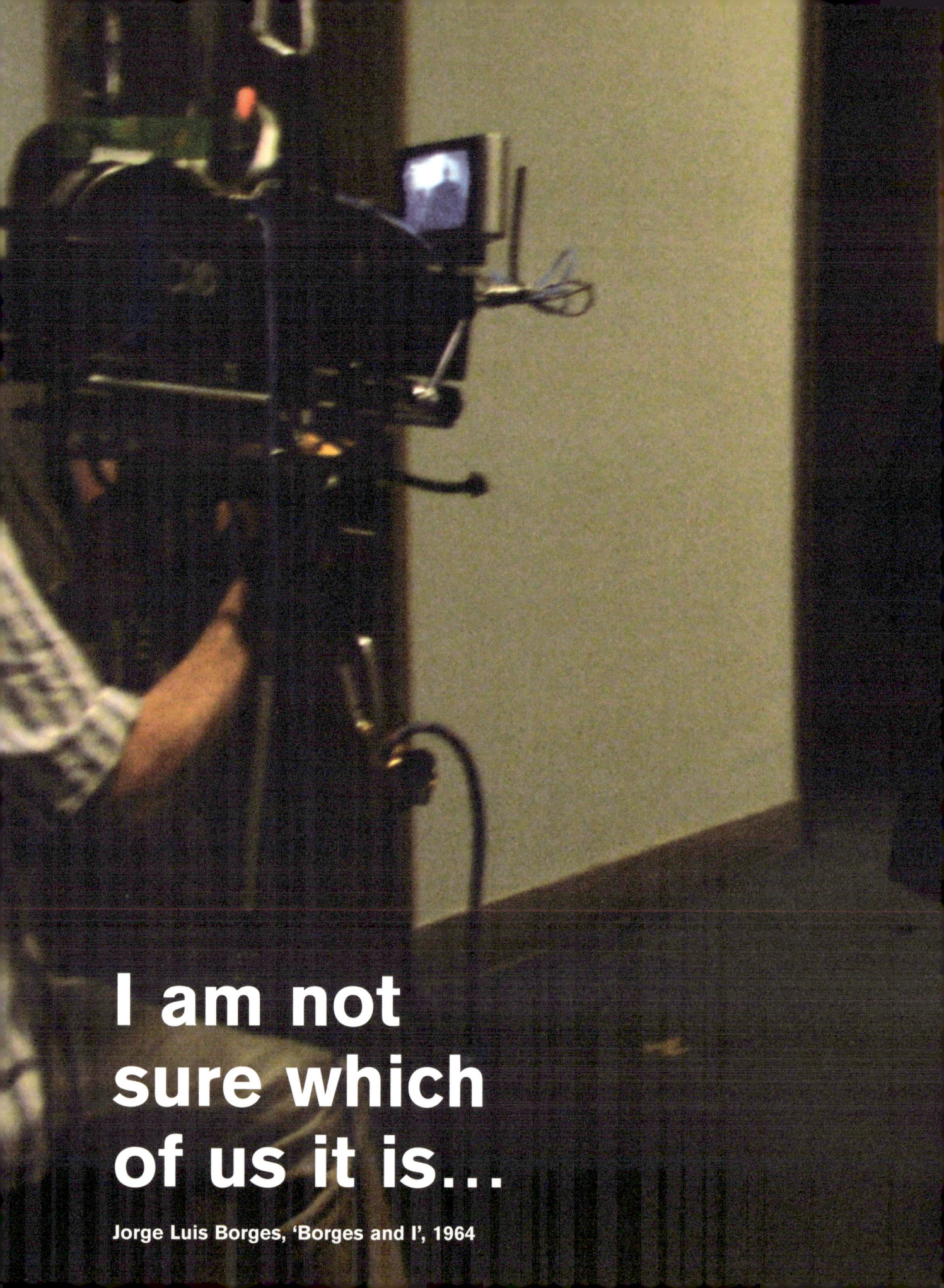

I am not
sure which
of us it is...

Jorge Luis Borges, 'Borges and I', 1964

and refer to an effect achieved 'out there', in the world of objects, producing, in other words, a 'fake', the curtain veiling the 'painting' achieves an effect 'in here', in the beholder's mind, and thus produces a 'truth': not about the world, but about this mind, its imagination, its desire and/or (self-) deception, which maybe too painful to confront, putting the viewer in a state of denial, or into the loop of (compulsive) repetition. In other words, Zeuxis and Parrhasios are two kinds of 'realists', whose strategies are, however, different and almost diametrically opposed, in the sense that the second is the meta-commentary on the first. It is not that Parrhasios is merely a 'baroque' trompe l'oeil realist against the classically representational Zeuxis. What matters is the interaction or interchange between the two, where Zeuxis' 'demand to see' mistakes Parrhasios' curtain as interposing itself between him and whatever he hopes to see represented. Zeuxis' category mistake *is* Parrhasios' painting, or put differently, whereas Zeuxis paints *grapes*, Parrhasios paints (the) *desire* (for grapes). Similarly, whereas some directors have filmed Marlene, Marilyn, or Madonna, Hitchcock has filmed the *desire* – for Madeleine, Melanie or Marnie.[37]

This doubling of mimesis by its own impossible desire for possession (and often fatal entanglement in the paradoxes of representation) points to another way of accounting for the mimetic pull in Hitchcock: the unexpected realism he engineers at the scale of detail (again, detail!) when the overall picture makes no sense at all: say, the minuscule lady's razor on Cary Grant's enormous jowl in the railway station washroom of *North by Northwest*. Accurate in itself, but misaligned in its proportions or settings, this is, of course, what makes an object hyper-real and a scene oneiric: such moments are the tipping points of mimesis, the ones practiced and perfected by the Surrealists. These switches, or parallax perceptions, are reinvented by Hitchcock in another idiom, and extended, one might argue, to include the plot. The endless fussing over minutiae, the obsession with getting the settings 'right' (which is to say, getting them from the register of verisimilitude into that of the absurdly improbable, by the tiniest of shifts in incident, like Marnie's shoe falling out of her coat-pocket, as she tiptoes away from Mark Rutland's safe), speak of the determination with which Hitchcock is said to have used and abused so many Hollywood screenwriters. The point was to arrive at a screenplay whose move and counter-move are invariably slung across an abyss, if we follow the self-cancelling logic of the MacGuffin. The solid strands of plotting that anchor character and motivation in the 'real world', yet leave so much unsaid and unspecified as to force the viewer to surmise most of it in his mind, serve to weave as dense a curtain as possible across the 'nothing there', or rather across the chuckling repartee that concludes the story of the famous device's origin: '(then) this is not a MacGuffin'.[38]

37 Žižek, who in a comment on the 'veiled Muslim women' debate in several European countries also refers to the Zeuxis/Parrhasios competition, draws an even bolder conclusion: 'And this brings us back to the function of veil in Islam: what if the true scandal this veil endeavours to obfuscate is not the feminine body hidden by it, but the *inexistence* of the feminine? What if, consequently, the ultimate function of the veil is precisely to sustain the illusion that there *is* something, the substantial Thing, behind the veil? If, following Nietzsche's equation of truth and woman, we transpose the feminine veil into the veil, which conceals the ultimate Truth, the true stakes of the Muslim veil become even clearer. Woman is a threat because she stands for the 'undecidability' of truth, for a succession of veils beneath which there is no ultimate hidden core; by veiling her, we create the illusion that there is, beneath the veil, the feminine Truth – the horrible truth of lie and deception, of course. Therein resides the concealed scandal of Islam: only a woman, the very embodiment of the indiscernability of truth and lie, can guarantee Truth. For this reason, she has to remain veiled.' (Slavoj Žižek, 'A Glance into the Archives of Islam': www.lacan.com/zizarchives.htm)

38 In the famous exchange between the two travellers, which Hitchcock tells Truffaut by way of explaining the origins of the MacGuffin, the final lines are: 'But: there *are* no lions in the Highlands!?' – 'Then, *this* is not a MacGuffin.'

Now you see it, now you don't: Magritte's Pipe and the Double, negative

The MacGuffin thus conceived suggests a revision to the idea of the mimetic pull, providing first an ontological gap that could suck one into a black hole, while also complicating it by the re-appearance of the Double, materialisation of this gap, and its always already implicit negative: the non-identity of this world with its own felt presence. And besides, 'Then, this is not ...' is, of course, itself the double of: 'Ceci n'est pas ...'. It repeats perhaps the most famous gesture of indexical negation, the line written by René Magritte into his advertment (or school-primer) drawing of a pipe, with the word/image combination creating an endlessly reversible rebus puzzle, or 'switch' (the painting is called: 'the treachery of images'). If we follow Foucault's commentary on 'Ceci n'est pas une pipe': at stake is the distinction between resemblance and similitude in visual representation. When implying that an image *resembles* reality, one assumes the ontological superiority of the latter. This is indeed what Magritte forestalls with the negative, rather than merely saying something as obvious as that you cannot smoke a painted pipe. With *similitude*, there is no originary referent, however much we might fantasise one: according to Foucault, things and images are 'more or less "like" each other without either of them able to claim the privileged status of model.' But Magritte not only breaks with resemblance, while apparently sticking to its representational rules. He also flouts another principle of classical painting: that the space of representation (the picture) and the space of writing or linguistic reference (the title) be separate and hierarchically subordinated to each other. What Magritte achieves by placing the words 'inside' (but why not 'on top of' or merely 'in'?) the painting and phrasing them in the negative is to create an oscillation or a hesitation, a kind of 'thrilling' of our perceptual norms and habitual expectations. These norms imply that perceiving, recognising and comprehending a two-dimensional image as a depiction of space requires an act of associative seeing, whereby optical and tactile, as well as linguistic and cognitive registers all work together, to confirm and synthesise the different sensory input. By separating the senses from each other, and putting them under the sign of negation, Magritte makes us aware of the 'division of labour' among their respective registers, while also bringing into play all kinds of traps for the mind and the eye that lurk in the folds of visual representation. The subtle, but excessive self-evidence of bourgeois order in Magritte – the tailored suits, the bowler hats, the umbrellas and other accessories or accoutrements of a regulated life are thus so many pointers to the mode of representation which his pictures at once instantiate and forever destroy. Many of Magritte's most typical effects are thus referenced to the basic issue of perspectival painting (but also cinema): how to depict a three-dimensional

...he's Alfred.

Alfred Hitchcock Presents, Episode #88: The Diplomatic Corpse,
broadcast on December 8, 1957

space on a two-dimensional surface. What he puts in crisis, for instance, are the signifiers of spatial depth, such as figure-ground relationships, perceptual cues with respect to light source and shadowing, the scale and positioning of objects within a perspectival image-space, or the direction of the characters' looks in relation to each other: meant to meet in mutual confirmation and yet destined forever to miss their (ap)point(ment)s of intersection, and instead vanishing into horizonless voids.

Obviously, it would be hard to substantiate a one-to-one correlation between Magritte's techniques and Hitchcock's plotting or framing, but the 'this is not …' formula gives a clue to their kinship, suggesting that a separation of the sensory registers and the production of cognitive dissonances may well be a factor in the kinds of uncanny each is able to achieve in his respective medium. If we do indeed take selective input from our perceptual field and create our own cognitive coherence – matching what we see with what we hear and with other perceptual cues, letting the brain take the strain of making it fit – then the slight mis-alignments Hitchcock habitually produces in his own solid worlds of middle-class mores are what brings about the peculiar mobilisation of the body, pulling us into the picture as a kind of supplement, at once necessary and in excess: which is itself a definition of the monstrative and the negative that come together in the indexical gesture asserting that 'this is not…'.

THIS IS NOT ALFRED HITCHCOCK

The phantom double stepping into this breach – necessary when he is not there and excessive when he appears – is the lookalike, apparently healing the rift, but in fact, also deepening it. Everything said so far: about the too many Hitchcocks of academia, about the Sphinx-like posture he occupies in the Oedipal scenarios of his critics, about his fatal attraction to artists and other world-makers, about Parrhasios' painted veil and the mimetic pull one feels before his films, finally points to nothing else: that Hitchcock is most himself when he can point to or index himself and say 'this is not Alfred Hitchcock', as he so often did, when stepping 'out of' the cinema and, for instance, 'into' television.

Looking for… (the 'real') Alfred is thus a productively futile exercise in more senses than one. First of all, because Hitchcock's (diegetic) presence in his films, through the walk-in cameo parts, at once in-side, out-side and be-side his creations, disavows his God-like control and thereby re-asserts it the more incontrovertibly, with the ontological knot being tied by what Bellour has called 'Hitchcock the enunciator',[39] but which I am now suggesting has also to do with 'Hitchcock the indicator': the invariably implied gesture of pointing. Not (only) voyeurism or scoptophilia is his trademark, but the metaphoric index finger,

39 See footnote 30.

Wait a minute... You've got the wrong man.

Alfred Hitchcock Presents, Episode #60: Number Twenty-two, **broadcast on February 17, 1957**

along which our spectatorial vision is led, as it were, by the nose, towards those divergent-dissonant vanishing points that make up the 'treachery of images'. They remind us all too palpably of our awkwardly real bodies, in what has been called Hitchcock's effects of 'motor mimicry',[40] or they propel us into his universe as if by gusts of wind, carrying us along, like dry leaves, before a downpour.

Productively futile also, because this 'looking for' has to be a 'casting around', rehearsing and repeating the founding gesture of the necessary excess, and following therein the (paratactic) logic of similitude rather than the (hierarchical) order of resemblance in representation, the latter's truth supposedly sustained and guaranteed 'from outside'. The lookalikes are thus of the order of 'similitude' rather than 'resemblance', for it is this order of similitude which ensures that the world of Hitchcock can appear more real than the real world, while being so self-confidently artificial: the 'piece of cake' rather than 'the slice of life', as Hitchcock notoriously put it. If the lookalikes acknowledge the (minimal) gap of all representational regimes, their serial similitude (as in Magritte), ensures the mise-en-abyme of (filmic) representation in two-dimensional space. By casting for the part, as it were, they preserve that moment of hesitation and oscillation on which is founded but also flounders our fascination for 'the Hitchcock moment': neither Aristotelian identification, nor Brechtian distanciation can here negotiate the dialectic of appearance and reality, and instead, it is the possibility of a double, *our* double, that haunts each of these (p)lunges, making them at once unreal and too real. From this apparition, this spectralisation of ourselves, in the act of seeing, the lookalike rescues or protects us, as the fake-double, being a sort of ontological scapegoat, in the guise of a fetish. How fortunate, therefore, that they do in fact exist, these Hitchcock lookalikes, and in so many preposterous, improbable or near perfect embodiments! They prove that the 'right man' has to be the 'wrong man' (and vice versa), in order to sustain the parallax vision, or 'partition' that marks the space where (not only) Hitchcock has just turned a corner: a whole hauntology of realism and reference, in its absence, is destined to still command the scene.

40 For 'motor mimicry' in Hitchcock, see Christine Noll-Brinckmann, 'Somatische Empathie bei Hitchcock: Eine Skizze', in: H.B. Heller / K. Prümm / D. Reulings (eds), 'Der Körper im Bild: Schauspielen – Darstellen – Erscheinen', Marburg (1999), pp. 111–121.

I remembered reading once that the best place to hide a leaf is in the forest.

Jorge Luis Borges, 'The Book of Sand', 1975

He's always th

Ron Burrage, Hitchcock double

ere, isn't he?

The Hitchcock Castings

Los Angeles

April 19/20, 2004
5225 Wilshire Boulevard
Suite 718

Emily Schweber Casting

From: Johan Grimonprez
To: Emily Schweber
Date: Wednesday, April 14, 2004 7:36 PM
Subject: Re: Hi, Beard

Well, a hitchcock on the set with a moustache would not be possible.
johan

> From: Emily Schweber
> Date: Wed, 14 Apr 2004 11:32:47 -0700
> To: Johan Grimonprez
> Subject: Re: Hi
>
> Question:
> If someone has a moustache or beard, would they have to shave?
>

From: Emily Schweber
To: Johan Grimonprez
Date: Monday, April 12, 2004 3:06 PM
Subject: Re: Nowcasting

I found a woman who looks like Alfred.

How much time for each appointment? 15 minutes?

> From: Johan Grimonprez
> Date: Thu, 08 Apr 2004 13:54:44 -0400
> To: Emily Schweber
> Subject: Re: Nowcasting
>
> Emily,
>
> Andrij Parekh, our DP is arriving on Monday the 19th around 9am at LAX
> airport. Would there be a possibility that we start on monday by 11 am,
> 11h30am? Tuesday the 20th for the call-back-day would not be a
> problem.
> I'll be in L.A. from thursday night on and if you like we could hook up on
> friday the 16th to go over some stuff and it would be great if i could check
> out the space on beforehand.
>
> All best,
>
>
> Johan
>

THE SUNDAY TIM
Is sin good?
Your husband or your life
Brilliant Brazil
Sale of £70m British house breaks world record
HEINZ
TOMATO KETCHUP

"LOOKING FOR ALFRED"

PLEASE SIGN IN. WE'LL BE WITH YOU SOON.

Paul Hayes and Morris J. Seawright, Hitchcock doubles

BIRD LEGS WALK
IN FRONT OF
CAMERA!!

NOT THAT
IMPORTANT
could be shot on 3rd day

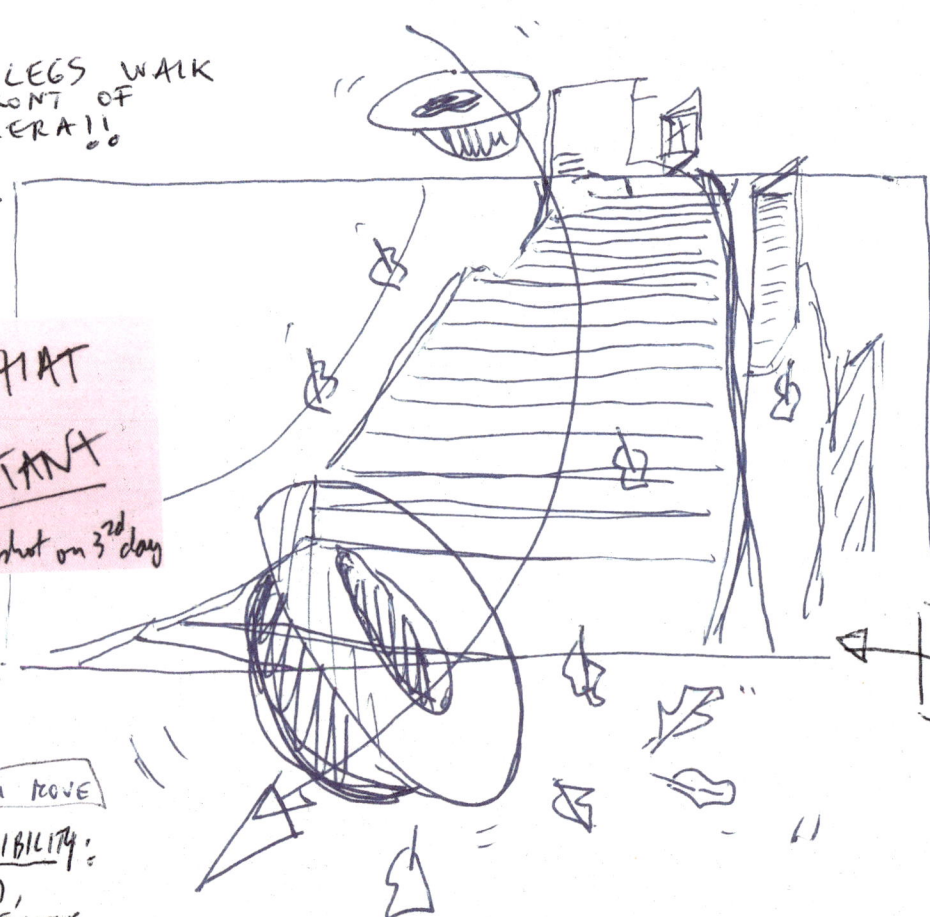

CAMERA:
- STATIC WITH MOVE
- ~~STATIC~~
- THIRD POSSIBILITY:
  HANDHELD,
  CAMERA FOLLOWS
  HAT TUMBLING
  DOWN THE STAIRS

Scene   Shot   Location

5

red couches
(green carpet
corridor)

- narrow door:
  red corridor
  + all light out
  (DARK)
  or : backlight
- green reflective
  = backlit corridor

...3x. EXTRA. HITCH
...(RON. SLEEPING ?)
....
....

- LEAVES + WIND MACHINE
- 3x 'HEGEL'S·HOLIDAY – UMBRELLAS'
- 3x HATS   + CIGARS ?
- contrala against wall

(plastic bag w/ eggs)

Shot description FOLLOW 3 HITCH COCKS
W/ BOWLER & 'HEGEL'S·HOLIDAY – UMBRELLAS' FROM THE BACK
DOWN THE STAIRS AND INTO THE ARCHED
CORRIDOR DISAPPEARING BEHIND ANGLE
OR DOOR INTO THE DARK

having cleaning HITCH here + SAFETY CONE

Plastic bag w/ eggs w hegel'n?

FOLLOW HITCHES
HANDHELD
DISAPPEAR IN THE DARK
OF A CORRIDOR – DOOR
OR BEHIND AN ANGLE

ghting

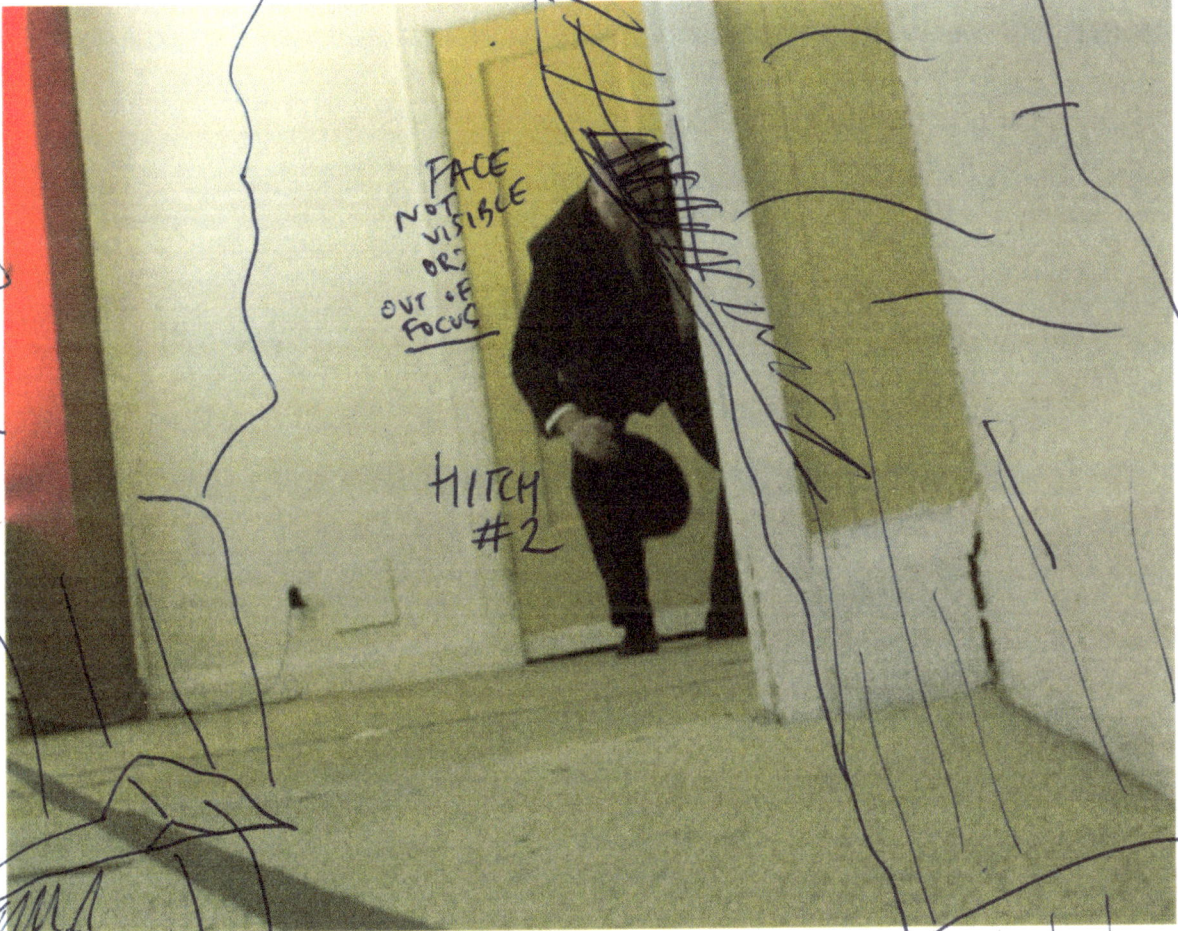

FACE
NOT
VISIBLE
OR
OUT OF
FOCUS

HITCH
#2

HITCH #1

Johan Grimonprez and Morgan Fredrix, Hitchcock double

Those of you who watched our broadcast of October 27, 1957 will remember that four minutes were lost due to a power failure. You'll be glad to hear that those four minutes have been found. They were discovered just west of Billings, Montana by an elderly prospector, who unfortunately used three of those minutes to softboil an egg, however he has returned the other minute…

…a minute called: 'tedious'. [ad follows]

Alfred Hitchcock in *The Alfred Hitchcock Hour, Episode #36: You'll be the death of me*, broadcast October 18, 1963

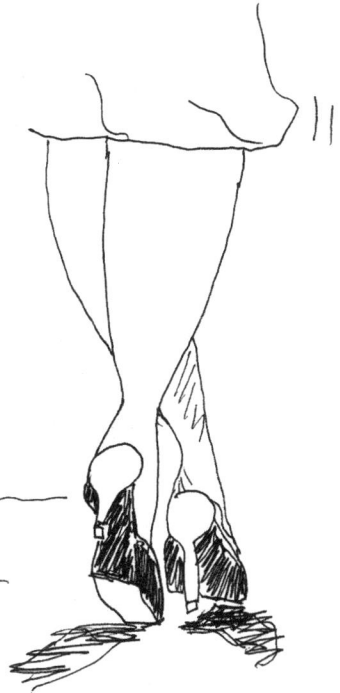

We were using a black-and-tan terrier who quietly vanished halfway through the film. It was imperative that we replace him for further scenes, but the new dog had to be an exact replica. We did the best we could. The new dog was made up to resemble the missing hound and even had a false tail stuck on. The difficulty arose when, the dog's dignity being offended, he proceeded to lick off all the make-up between shots!

Alfred Hitchcock on shooting *The Pleasure Garden* in 'Hitchcock on Hitchcock: Selected Writings and Interviews', ed. Sidney Gottlieb

Zale Kessler, Hitchcock double
Brussels, 2004, shoot for *Looking for Alfred*

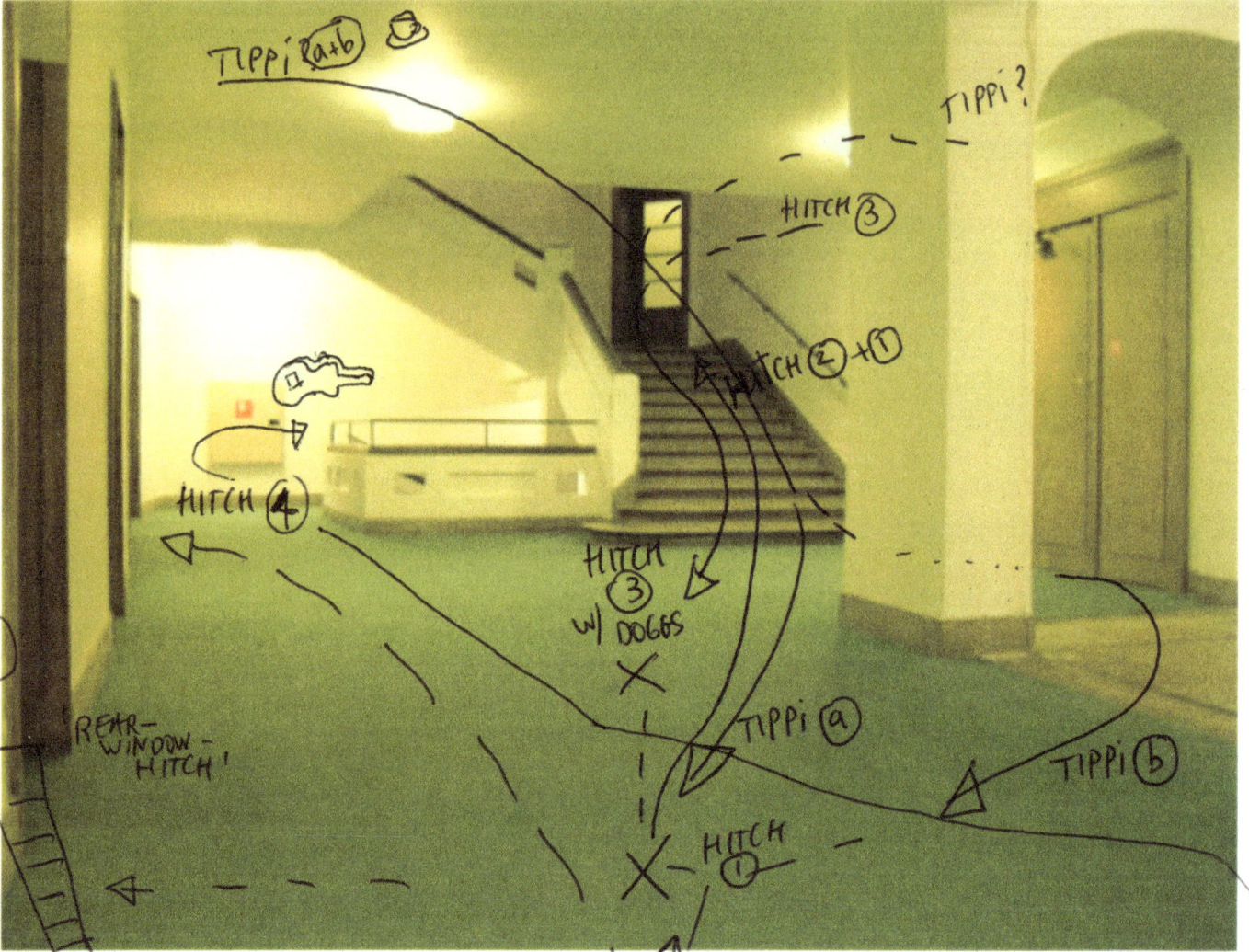

Scene   Shot   Location

⑨	①	arcade (stairs)

Cast required
1. ...tippi............
2. ...hitch 3... w/...dogs in the back *following*
3. ...hitch 1.............. → *passing by*
4. ... hitch 4 ...... → *disappear in background*
5.   rear-window hitch → *on the ~~left~~ right*

Art direction and props .. bird cage .. + ...saucer... *coffee & 2 spoon*
.... - umbrella + hat + ...2 dogs.....
.... [.. leaves .. + .. wind machine ..] *?*

① top view seeing two floors → *choreography?*

Shot description ② ~~top view of stairs : tippi~~
BACKWARDS TRACKING OF TIPPI'S FEET ...descends... and a little after that hitch 3 w/
....his dogs.. Leaves blow in on the highest
.....floor only, a couple blow down the stairs.
.....A little later ~~hitch 1~~ walks up the stairs.

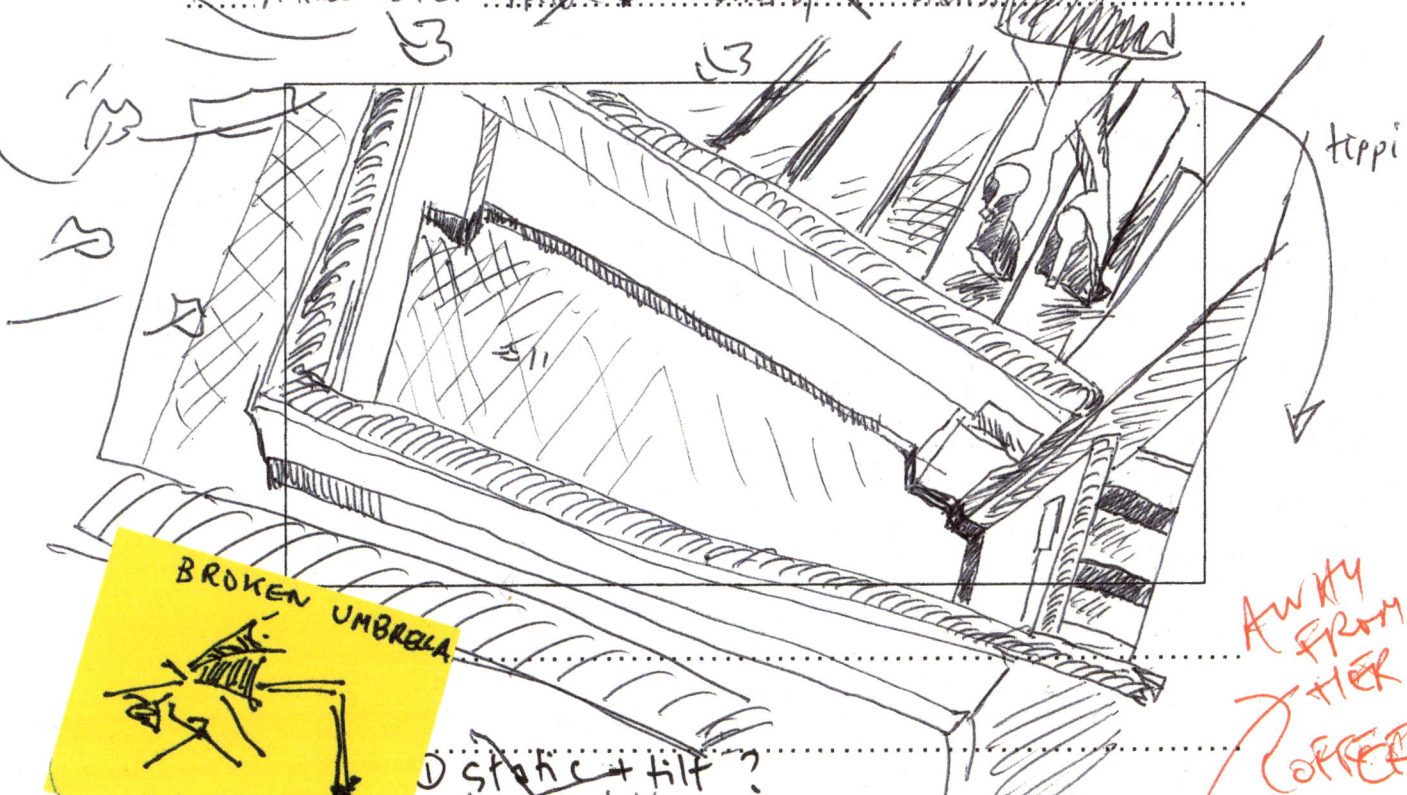

BROKEN UMBRELLA

tippi

AWAY FROM HER COFFEE

① static + tilt ?
② static + tilt top view of stairs

① *CU Tippi's feet on stairs + CU eyes on stairs glance to her*
② *BACKWARDS TRACKING OF STAIRS coffee*

If I was making 'Cinderella,' everyone would look for the corpse. And if Edgar Allan Poe had written 'Sleeping Beauty', one would look for the murderer.

'Why I am Afraid of the Dark' in 'Hitchcock on Hitchcock: Selected Writings and Interviews', ed. Sidney Gottlieb

Delfine Bafort
Looking for Alfred, 2004

I've always dreamed of
a murder in a tulip field.
Two characters: the killer
behind the girl,
his victim. As his shadow
creeps up on her, she
turns and screams.
Immediately, we pan
down to the struggling
feet in the tulip field.
One petal fills the
screen, and suddenly a
drop of blood splashes
all over it.

Alfred Hitchcock in François Truffaut,
'Hitchcock Interviews', Touchstone Edition,
Simon & Schuster, New York, 1983

'Where would a

a leaf?' 'In the f

'But what does

is no forest?'

'Well, well,' crie

irritably, 'what c

'He grows a for

G. K. Chesterton, 'The Sign of the Broken Sword',
from 'Father Brown Short Stories', 1911

wise man hide

rest.'

ne do if there

l Flambeau

oes he do?'

st to hide it in.'

1.b

zZZZ → later

heef CELLO?

 LIGHTS CIGAR

 etc.

SHOESTORE

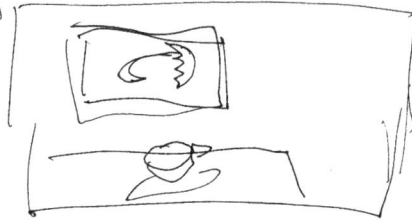

FAST FOOD RESTOS

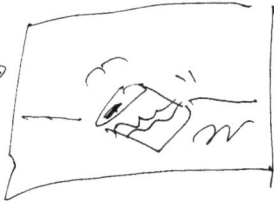

→ H jaauway

#17 visual key FOLLOW SHOES

GUM WRAPPER

CITY STREET SOUND + just FOOTSTEPS

later on her

appears behind wall

SURVEILLANCE

FedEx

Scene   Shot   Location

15

1.

4.

BUS STOP
ALFRED-H- HOTEL

Cas

TRY
surveillance
Montrose blvd
check if
useable?

Art direction and props

y dad getting
on the bus
w/ contractors

Shot description .....H.I.T.CH....M.....

→ bus

"SHOP
SOMEWHERE
ELSE"

HX10

"North x Northwest"
(1959)

Randall Bosley and Zale Kessler, Hitchcock doubles

I've kissed ass, but I never missed a bus to get a part in a movie!

Randall Bosley, on the restaging of Hitchcock's
North by Northwest cameo, missing the bus on Wilshire Boulevard
Hitchcock casting, Los Angeles, June 2004

Dial M for Magritte

Patricia Allmer

That day it was twice Monday…

René Magritte, 'Écrits Complets'

Dial M for Magritte

PATRICIA ALLMER

'We are like twins, don't you see?'
(*Shadow of a Doubt*, 1943)

La Reproduction interdite (*Not to be Reproduced*) (1937) is one of the most archetypal of René Magritte's paintings. It shows a man standing in front of a mirror, in which the mirror image has gone awry – rather than reflecting the man, it reproduces, in apparent disavowal of the painting's title, the same image of the man's back as constitutes the painting. The only thing accurately reflected is the cover of Edgar Allan Poe's book 'The Narrative of Arthur Gordon Pym of Nantucket' (1838), which is shown in this painting in its French edition, a translation from 1857 by Charles Baudelaire as 'Aventures d'Arthur Gordon Pym'. Poe's novel offers a narrative which is like a Chinese box, revealing endless layers of meta-narrators, echoing the back-view of the man in Magritte's painting where, although the person is reproduced, his real identity is never revealed. In Poe's novel, at the moment we seem to be able to work out who the narrator is, another meta-voice occurs, leaving just a chimera, a brief glimpse of the previous narrator's identity. Magritte's painting misidentifies the mirror image, offering, instead of a conventional reflection, a repetition: it repeats rather than reflects, and seems to lead us back to a primal scene, a re-visitation (or reproduction) of the Lacanian mirror stage which consists of the foundational misidentification of the subject with its reflection in the mirror. Magritte's painting, or at least the interdiction of its title, appears to constitute a warning, a correction of the Lacanian subject's misidentification – his painting's misidentification of the mirror image as repetition rather than a reflection, is, in a strange way, the correction of the subject's misidentification in the mirror stage, pointing out that the mirror image *is not* the subject *per se*, but a 'repetition', a copy.

The implication of this painting is that there is no original – that the world of images is a world comprised of copies lacking a basis in originality, where originality is closely connected to identity. *Not to be Reproduced* inculcates what Michel Foucault referred to in Magritte's art as 'similitude' as opposed to 'resemblance', where serial repetitions undermine notions of an original. Foucault argues that Magritte's work dissociates, through methods of doubling, similitude from resemblance – whilst resemblance always points to a 'model', an original element. Foucault argues: 'To me it appears that Magritte dissociated similitude

René Magritte, *La Reproduction interdite*, 1937. Oil on canvas, 81 x 65 cm
Museum Boijmans van Beuningen, Rotterdam

from resemblance, and brought the former into play against the latter. Resemblance has a "model", an original element, that orders and hierarchises the increasingly less faithful copies that can be struck from it. Resemblance presupposes a primary reference that prescribes and classes. The similar develops in series that have neither beginning nor end […] that obey no hierarchy, but propagate themselves from small differences among small differences.'[1] Foucault reveals Magritte's art practice as being based on similitude and not on resemblance. Similitude in this argument undermines the traditional notions of representation (which seeks affirmation outside of itself) and the hierarchies introduced by them. Copies here are copies from previous copies, the affirmative in similitude is denied. Representations of objects stay locked up in representation and relate to other representations, but never pretend or desire to reach outside of themselves – indeed *Not to be Reproduced* is not based on any original, but on a photographic portrait of Edward James, marking the lack of an original.

In Johan Grimonprez's *Looking for Alfred* (2004) the scene of *Not to be Reproduced* is re-staged, producing further doublings of this image, and sending it further awry. In *Looking for Alfred* a man is shown standing in front of a mirror putting a bowler hat on his head – once again we only see his back. However, the mirror does not reflect his front, but reproduces the image of the man's back, until that which we presupposed to be a mirror image walks out of the frame, adding a further layer to the erasure of the boundaries between 'original' and 'copy'. At the moment where the supposed mirror image walks out of the frame, we get a brief glance at his profile (reminiscent of the fleeting glimpses of the possible identity of Poe's meta-narrators). Although the title of Grimonprez's work is a bit of a giveaway, it isn't only that which encourages us to match his profile to the well-known silhouette of Alfred Hitchcock, whilst the other man, left standing in the mirror, resembles, through the angular shoulders of the suit, his short, sturdy neck and his bowlerhat, the archetypal back-view, familiar from this and other Magritte paintings. The two men are so much alike that they could be mirror images of each other, and yet the differences are marked out – the mirror image can exit the frame; can leave its other. Grimonprez's drawing together of Hitchcock and Magritte in *Looking for Alfred* seems to display a similar dynamic of belonging together, where one shares the contours of the other, yet is not, at the same time, at one with the other – implying those Hitchcockian figures who incorporate two distinct personalities, such as Norman Bates in *Psycho* (1960), Madeleine, 'that completely different woman who is nevertheless the same'[2] in *Vertigo* (1958), Manny Balestrero in *The Wrong Man* (1956), John Ballentine in *Spellbound* (1945), or Roger O. Thornhill in *North by Northwest* (1959).

In *Looking for Alfred*, a strange, hallucinatory dreamscape/crime-scene of

1 Michel Foucault, 'This is not a Pipe', London, University of California Press (1982), p.44.

2 Mladen Dolar, 'Hitchcock's Objects' in Slavoj Žižek (ed) 'Everything You Always Wanted to Know About Lacan… But Were Afraid to Ask Hitchcock', London, Verso (2000), p. 45.

metonymy and metaphor, of condensation and displacement, is created, where 'elective affinities' and 'dangerous liaisons' between the two masters of shock are explored and established – affinities and liaisons which simultaneously blur and more sharply outline the distinction between Magritte and Hitchcock. The Chiricoesque space of the Palais des Beaux-Arts in Brussels (which housed a monumental René Magritte exhibition in 2005, running in conjunction with the premiere of *Looking for Alfred* which was installed alongside the exhibition) becomes a space where Magritte's paintings, such as *Golconde* (1953) with its 'raining men', *Les Vacances de Hegel* (*Hegel's Holidays*) (1958), where a glass of water is balanced on an umbrella and, of course, *Not to be Reproduced*, showing a 'failed portrait'[3] reproduced from a photograph, are brought together with film scenes by Hitchcock, as well as outlining some of the striking resemblances between Magritte's paintings and Hitchcock's scenes – Gregory Peck as an amnesia case in *Spellbound* is literally a reference to the 'failed portrait', since his amnesia is compared to looking into a mirror and not seeing a face, or in *I Confess* (1953) where the prosecutor, Willy Robertson, balances a glass of water reminiscent of Magritte's painting of *Hegel's Holidays*. The colour scheme of Grimonprez's film mixes Magritte's pastel pinks and blues with the rich greens and reds of the Technicolor of Hitchcock's later films.

Grimonprez leads the viewer into a labyrinth of what Magritte called the 'shock of affinity', which he discovered in a key moment of awakening, and to which the 'shock of bringing together unrelated objects' (as was the case for example in the shock produced by Lautréamont's fortuitous encounter between an umbrella and a sewing machine on a dissecting table) had to give way. Magritte described that moment, which also features in his painting *La Clairvoyance* (1936), as follows: 'I awoke one night in my room, in which a cage with a sleeping bird was placed. A wonderful mistake allowed me to see in the cage an egg instead of the disappeared bird. With this I seized hold of a new and astonishing poetic secret, because the shock, which I experienced, was induced by the affinity of two objects – cage and egg, whilst previously this shock was induced by the encounter of objects foreign to each other.'[4]

In *Looking for Alfred* the shock of affinities, between Hitchcock and Magritte, occurs on a number of levels. The film's deeply oneiric scenes induce a series of associations between Magritte's paintings and Hitchcock's films – for example in the scene where the blonde girl innocently holds up a savaged dove whilst her mouth is smeared in what seems to be the dove's blood. The girl, who in other scenes carries a cage with a bird and a coffee cup and saucer, has obviously been modelled on Melanie Daniels from Hitchcock's *The Birds* (1963), (who, as well as being a bearer of love-birds, is characterised by her strangely

3 Paul Colinet categorised Magritte's constantly recurring paintings of the back view and the missing, obscured or concealed face as '*portraits manqué*' (failed portraits). See David Sylvester and Sarah Whitfield, (eds) 'René Magritte: Catalogue Raisonné II – Oil Paintings and Objects 1931–1948', London, Philip Wilson Publishers (1993), p. 244.

4 René Magritte 'La Ligne de Vie I' (1938) in André Blavier (ed) 'René Magritte: Écrits Complets', Paris, Flammarion (2001), p. 110. (My translation)

repeated handling of crockery), while her blood-smeared lips and the dying dove in her hands evoke Magritte's *Jeune fille mangeant un oiseau (Le Plaisir)* (*Girl Eating a Bird [Pleasure]*) (1927).

The blonde girl's own body is a map of struggling affinities. She is a collaged figure (an exquisite corpse?), an accumulation of different Hitchcockian and Magrittean women – her meticulously shaped, long, red nails seem to imitate those of Melanie Daniels, whilst her hair-style and face are reminiscent of Eve Kendall in *North by Northwest*; her appearance with a dove echoes Magritte's portrait of a nude with a dove on her shoulders called *La Magie Noire (Black Magic)* (1934), and her posture, clothing and innocent expression evoke 'Alice in Wonderland'. The figure of Alice also occurs in various forms in *The Birds* – the shopkeeper, when trying to think of the name of Mitch's sister, Cathy, for example, misremembers her as Alice. Camille Paglia associates the key moment of the film where Melanie turns from predator to prey, a moment before her head is made to bleed by the attack of a seagull (an image reminiscent of Magritte's *La Memoir* [*Memory*] (1948), where a sculpted female head bleeds from its right temple), with a scene from 'Alice in Wonderland':

> When he catches sight of the boat, she sits up and tries to start the motor. It takes six yanks to do it, and the hacking, hesitating sputters may suggest that her penetration and control of the physical world are about to end. Indeed, at this moment, squawking gulls fly for the first time into the frame. Mitch dashes back into the house and emerges with binoculars – for battle or bird-watching. [...] This scene always reminds me of that moment when Carroll's 'Alice', sitting in a train compartment with a talking goat and a gentleman dressed in white paper, is inspected by a guard through a telescope, a microscope, and opera-glasses. Mitch, pulling Melanie into focus, is like Hitch the director, baffled and bemused by women and contemplating them across the wide wastes of gender.[5]

Magritte's comment on *Girl Eating a Bird* also calls to mind Alice and other female characters who seem to incorporate their authors' and creators' fears, such as Poe's 'Eleonora' (1841) and 'Berenice' (1835): 'We find her in the heart of summer, in the shade of a sturdy tree thronged with calm birds unalarmed by her presence. Her school-girl demeanour would be excuse enough, and her modest dress, her neat hair. It is a familiar picture, an unremarkable encounter in the countryside. But the pallor of the face surprises, and arrests attention. Those half-closed eyes, that tilted head, are not so simple.'[6] The blonde girl in *Looking*

5 Camille Paglia 'The Birds', London, bfi Publishing (1998), p. 16.

6 David Sylvester and Sarah Whitfield (eds) 'René Magritte: Catalogue Raisonné I – Oil Paintings 1916–1930', London, Philip Wilson Publishers (1992), pp. 216–217.

5,000 sparrows,
3,000 crows,
800 swallows,
150 robins,
and 2 lovebirds:
yes, Mr. Hitchcock,
we can arrange that.

Alfred Hitchcock joke

for Alfred is a similarly dark version of Alice. She is an *alter ego* who has, like the mirror image from its 'object' in Grimonprez's loop, detached herself from Hitchcock's assigned role of 'tormented woman' at the edge of a nervous breakdown[7] and returns as an ethereal collective to haunt 'the master'. The tables are turned – she is now in charge of the crockery, which once signified the fragility of her mind (*The Birds*)[8], and which was brought to her in a number of films as associated with potential acts of poisoning (as in the case of the poisoned teacup in *Notorious* [1946] or the seemingly poisoned glass of milk in *Suspicion* [1941]). Now, in Grimonprez's loop, she ardently returns the poisoned cup to Hitchcock, and her devouring of the dove suggests that the birds do not torment her any more, do not tear the flesh off her body any longer as if impatiently trying to reveal what is underneath it, but rather are there, as in the case of the crow, to watch, haunt and shadow Hitchcock's every move, as the cat in Poe's 'The Black Cat' (1843).

The associations unfold further and create wider and wider circles – the letter 'M', for example, was important to both Hitchcock and Magritte. Hitchcock constantly returned to names and words beginning with this letter, in central characters like Mitch ('Hitch' starting with an 'M'); Madeleine and Marjorie (*Vertigo*); Mark and *Marnie* (1964); Ann Morton, and Metcalf (the first letter of which is mirrored in Washington) (*Strangers on a Train*, 1951); Marion, Motel and Mother (*Psycho*) or Manny and Mama Balestrero in *The Wrong Man*. The letter M always seems to find its destination in Hitchcock, be it in M for Murder, Mirror, Motif, Maniac, Marriage and Madness (the bowler hat, by the way, is *Melone* in German and *chapeau melon* in French) – not to forget the most important 'M', the MacGuffin – the joke which plays on the conflation of boundaries between the meaningful and the meaningless. And then there is Magritte, with his jokes about his name being similar to George Simenon's bowler hat-wearing, pipe-smoking detective Maigret, and Dalí's less fond misnaming of him as Margerite. All this recalls the professor's remark, in *North by Northwest*, to Roger O. Thornhill, alias George Kaplan: 'We're all in the same alphabet soup.'

Both Hitchcock and Magritte inscribed themselves and their family members in their artworks – Hitchcock and his daughter, Patricia, repeatedly appeared in cameos; Magritte himself and his wife, Georgette, repeatedly appeared in his paintings. Hitchcock inscribed his initials into his films, for example in the name Annie Hayworth in *The Birds* or Alicia Huberman in *Notorious* (1946), as well as his wife's first name, such as in the character of Alma Keller in *I Confess*. Similarly Magritte repeatedly placed his signature so that it became integral rather than external to the art work, not least in the painting *La Trahison des images* (*The Treachery of Images*) (1928) where the statement 'This is not a pipe'

7 The characters' torment was often carried over into the filming itself – Tippi Hedren was injured several times and collapsed in exhaustion during the filming of *The Birds*, and described the filming of the attic scene as 'the worst week of my life'). Paglia, p.16.

8 See Ibid., p. 60.

also challenges the status of the artist's signature and its authoritative character. More affinities between Hitchcock and Magritte begin to surface – both utilise mirrors and birds in their respective artistic productions. In one of Magritte's 'failed' self-portraits called *Le Thérapeute* (*The Healer*) (1937) a birdcage with two birds (doves and not love-birds) has replaced his body. Hitchcock appears with his two white terriers (typically British dogs) in his cameo in *The Birds*, whilst Magritte's child-substitutes were small Spitzes, the last of which in the sixties was a black Schipperke (a typically Belgian dog) and both had a smoking instrument, a cigar or a pipe, as their characteristic motif – Hitchcock's trademark was a cigar and Magritte famously painted a pipe in 1928 underneath which loomed the inscription *Ceci n'est pas une pipe* (*This is not a pipe*).

Perhaps the clearest manifestation of this 'shock of affinities' is in Grimonprez's uniting of the figures (or signifiers) of Magritte and Hitchcock in the character of the bowler-hatted man, who is enacted by numerous Hitchcock doubles (or are they Magritte? – the double has already doubled). Both Hitch and Magritte wore bowler hats and conventional suits to assume the personae of somewhat droll, two-dimensional bourgeois figures with conventional family lives. The bowler-hatted man in *Looking for Alfred* evokes Magritte's numerous paintings of this bourgeois Modernist character. Magritte himself took on the role of the bowler-hatted man, doubling his painterly others, similar to Hitchcock's cameos which acted as mirrors or doubles of the storyteller (Hitchcock made a bowler-hatted cameo appearance in *Frenzy* [1972]), in order to 'conflate the images of artist and bowler-hatted man.'[9] The bowler-hatted man in Magritte's art has a number of sources, ranging from crime mysteries such as Victorin Jasset's *Nick Carter* (1908 – 1912) and Louis Feuillade's *Judex* cycle (1916 – 1917) to Charlie Chaplin's[10] bowler hat and his typical back-view silhouette, which seemed particularly to influence the 'failed portrait' element in Magritte's bowler hats.[11]

The bowler-hatted man has generally been seen as an 'abomination to the individualist'.[12] It became a sign of 'black-clad, mechanized, *replicable* men, all middle-class'[13] with 'featureless faces'[14] – a mistaken view indeed, as pointed out by Magritte, commenting on *Golconde*: 'there is a crowd of men, different men. But since one doesn't think of an individual in a crowd, the men are dressed the same, as simply as possible, to indicate a crowd.'[15] As Miller Robinson suggests, the 'error is to simplify'[16] this character, or to underestimate this anonymously appearing man, since the biggest fictional detectives and criminals, ranging from the Belgian detective Hercule Poirot to Fantômas, have deceived through their inconspicuous appearance, through apparently being just another 'man of the crowd', just like Hitchcock in his cameos, granting the fool-proof

9 Fred Miller Robinson, 'The Man in the Bowler Hat: His History and Iconography', London, The University of North Carolina Press (1993), pp. 140 – 141.

10 Chaplin himself entered a lookalike contest in which he ended third.

11 Peter Wollen 'Magritte and the Bowler Hat', 'New Left Review' 1, January / February 2000, p. 109.

12 Miller Robinson, p. 26.

13 Ibid.

14 Ibid., p. 125.

15 René Magritte, interview for 'Life', 1966, in Sylvester *et al*, p. 205.

16 Miller Robinson, p. 127.

freedom of a Charlie Chaplin. A photograph of 1938 depicts Magritte miming the figure of Fantômas in his painting *Le Barbare*, a character whose main feature is that he can slip in and out of roles and appear in many different bourgeois identities. Fantômas is the master criminal who subverts the everyday, by slipping into the role of its actors. Which position is pursued by Magritte – is he '*le grand détective*' or is he Fantômas? As is well known, successful criminals and detectives in literature are not dissimilar to each other – is Hitchcock the one who constructs the crime or he who solves the crime? And Grimonprez – is he trying to reveal their complicity or is he complicit too?

The bowler-hatted man in *Looking for Alfred* unites Magritte and Hitchcock, leading the viewer deeper and deeper into a search for something which is not. The bowler-hatted Hitchcock/Magritte lookalikes, being trapped in time, double up on each other, eternally picking up the abandoned bowler hat like a theatrical cue to character. Grimonprez's use of doubles establishes another, perhaps *the* most significant, link between Hitchcock and Magritte – both made heavy use of strategies of doubling and duplication – 'criss-cross', as Bruno would say in *Strangers on a Train*, a film in whose opening shots we 'get the symmetrical presentation of two pairs of shoes that we follow from a taxi to a carriage; the shot of rails, parallel and inevitably intersecting in the distance, just as the shoes will inevitably bump into each other, thus linking another pair, Guy and Bruno, fatally bound together.'[17] This couple forms the axis for further duplications in the film: 'there are two towns […], two ladies in Guy's life; two young men accompanying Miriam; […] two scenes at the funfair with two guardians and two little boys;'[18] – not to forget Hitchcock's cameo carrying a double bass, 'the instrument later played by the 'wrong man' Manny Balestrero.'[19] Similarly in *Shadow of a Doubt* (1943) the narrative evolves around the central axis of the relationship between Charlie (the niece) and Charlie (her uncle) which is described by the niece Charlie: 'We are like twins; we are both alike.'[20]

Duplication and doubling are also central elements in Magritte's art. He used the same title for different paintings and produced a number of paintings which were copies of previous ones. He also used a mostly limited range of icons and mise-en-scenes so that the same objects and settings duplicated in different artworks. Sometimes Magritte consorted to less legal forms of duplication, namely forgery.[21] Doubling was also a recurrent theme, since 1927, in a number of his paintings, some of which formed 'astounding "stereographic" compositions.'[22]

Magritte's painterly research was deeply immersed in questions and possibilities of re-presentation, of duplication. He commented: 'The resemblance of two eggs for example is called colloquially similarity: one says "being alike as two eggs". But one also says that "there are no absolutely identical eggs in this

17 Dolar, p. 39.

18 Ibid.

19 Ibid.

20 Ibid., p. 32.

21 See Patricia Allmer, '*La Reproduction Interdite* – René Magritte and Forgery', 'Papers of Surrealism', Issue 5, April 2007, www.surrealismcentre.ac.uk/ publications/papers/index.html

22 Patrick Roegiers, 'Magritte and Photography', Aldershot, Lund Humphries (2005), p. 39.

world" and indeed the two eggs are separate from each other, each has its own identity. The similarity, as it is called in colloquial speech, is more or less similar.'[23] Magritte's comment helps cast some light on Grimonprez's cast of lookalikes, who, far from resembling each other, differ sometimes quite significantly (Hitchcock, by the way, hated eggs because his father dealt in poultry – a neurosis which found expression in *The Birds*). Grimonprez's bowler-hatted man resembles those of Magritte and Hitchcock, but clearly differs from them too – the resemblance is approximate, a resemblance due to type rather than identity. Hitchcock also uses doublings and double-characters not to reveal their similarity, but their difference from each other. In *Looking for Alfred* the lookalikes are used not to mark resemblance but to emphasise difference, to draw the viewer's attention to resemblance at the level of type rather than identity. This is particularly clearly demonstrated by the climactic moment in the film where one of the Hitchcock/Magritte doubles turns round to reveal that he is a Chinese man, thus inducing the shock of radical dissimilarity in the midst of similarity. The loop emphasises the reliance of the 'failed portrait' on the viewer's tendency to stereotype (to assume resemblances).

The props of anonymity and uniformity provided by the figure of the bowler-hatted man, mean that the various doubles here lack an original from which they would derive. None of them could be taken as the 'model' for or the 'origin' of the others. Instead they mirror each other in a skewed, distorted way seemingly an endless enactment of reproduction. Similitude is introduced here into an endless play of simulacra; as Michel Foucault argues, it 'multiplies different affirmations, which dance together, tilting and tumbling over one another'[24] without beginning or end, returning to the beginning of the loop, circulating the 'simulacrum as an indefinite […] relation of the similar to the similar'[25] rather than trying to find an origin, a beginning, or impose hierarchical orders. Grimonprez's film as a whole could be compared to a mirror image gone awry, as in the scene reproducing Magritte's painting *Not to be Reproduced*, where what according to conventional logic should be the 'mirror image' exits the frame before the 'original', subverting and destroying the notional relation between original and mirror image. However, this moment of assertion of difference, a moment of 'being out of sync', like a slight shift of the eye, like a slight discord in a musical score, is also the very moment of revealing the similarity between Hitchcock and Magritte.

Grimonprez's play of similarities reveals the dissimilar, the 'this is not', so familiar from Magritte's famous painting of the pipe, where resemblances between the painted pipe and a real pipe, the painted pipe and the painted word 'pipe', are deconstructed through the term 'this is not', through the very inability

23 René Magritte 'La Ressemblance' (1959) in Blavier, p. 493. (My translation)

24 Foucault, p. 46.

25 Ibid.

of 'ceci' / 'this' to refer to one thing or another. Grimonprez follows this Magrittean logic, which Magritte himself also identified in Hitchcock's films, where 'white becomes black'[26], a logic which 'contradicts *de facto* the codified logic, without ever attacking it.'[27] The doubles warn us about misunderstanding reality and representation, one for the other, at the very moment they establish the affinities between the two – just as Magritte warns, in his sentence written in schoolmasterly form underneath the pipe, that 'This is not a pipe', and just as Bruno, in *Strangers on a Train*, has to learn that misunderstanding the relations between rhetorical codes and reality as constituting 'real' contracts is fatal. Both Hitchcock and Magritte are teaching us a lesson.

In *Looking for Alfred* the moment of revelation is not a moment of affirmation and confirmation, but rather exactly their limits, creating instead a moment where the loss of Hitchcock/Magritte becomes apparent and can be experienced – a moment which leaves 'as a trace its own absence.'[28] These doubles refer to 'nothing more than themselves,'[29] loosening further any notion of identity outside of their filmic realm and universe, like the MacGuffin which is, according to Slavoj Žižek, 'a pure semblance: in itself it is totally indifferent and, by structural necessity, absent; its signification is purely autoreflexive.'[30] The doubles, like the MacGuffin, 'signify only that they signify'[31] – they construct a universe in which assertions of identity and being through mirrors and key-signifiers cannot gain a foothold. The bowler-hatted men here are accompanied by Poe's raven, who marks the scene, silently croaking out 'Nevermore', exploring rather than masking the absence of Magritte and Hitchcock. This is also connoted by Grimonprez's title *Looking for Alfred*, looking for somebody who has been lost, recalling Magritte's first Surrealist painting *Le Jockey perdu* (*The Lost Jockey*) (1926).

Looking for Alfred is also strangely similar to Magritte's painting of *L'Homme au chapeau melon* (*The Man in the Bowler Hat*) (1964) – whilst the static man meets the dove in motion, Grimonprez's loop draws together (in a motion picture full of still images) Magritte, as the master of painterly stasis, with Hitchcock, the master of cinematic motion. The doubles in *Looking for Alfred* are comparable to the dove-in-flight frozen in front of the bowler-hatted man's face, which 'reminds us of what the man is not, and yet, in front of his face (is it frozen there forever? That is, is it *his*?) it becomes part of his expressive life, as distinct from his inexpressive style.'[32] Grimonprez's doubles behave just like the dove in front of the bowler-hatted man's face, forming, perhaps, the only legitimate act of homage, of acknowledging and revealing (through hiding) that which is absent – they are the representatives of void, endless doubles of themselves, of the MacGuffin, the 'nothing at all'.

26 René Magritte, letter to André Bosmans (23 July 1960) in Blavier, p. 148. (My translation)

27 Ibid.

28 Foucault, p. 54.

29 Ibid.

30 Slavoj Žižek, 'Introduction', in Žižek, p. 6.

31 Dolar, p. 45.

32 Miller Robinson, p. 127.

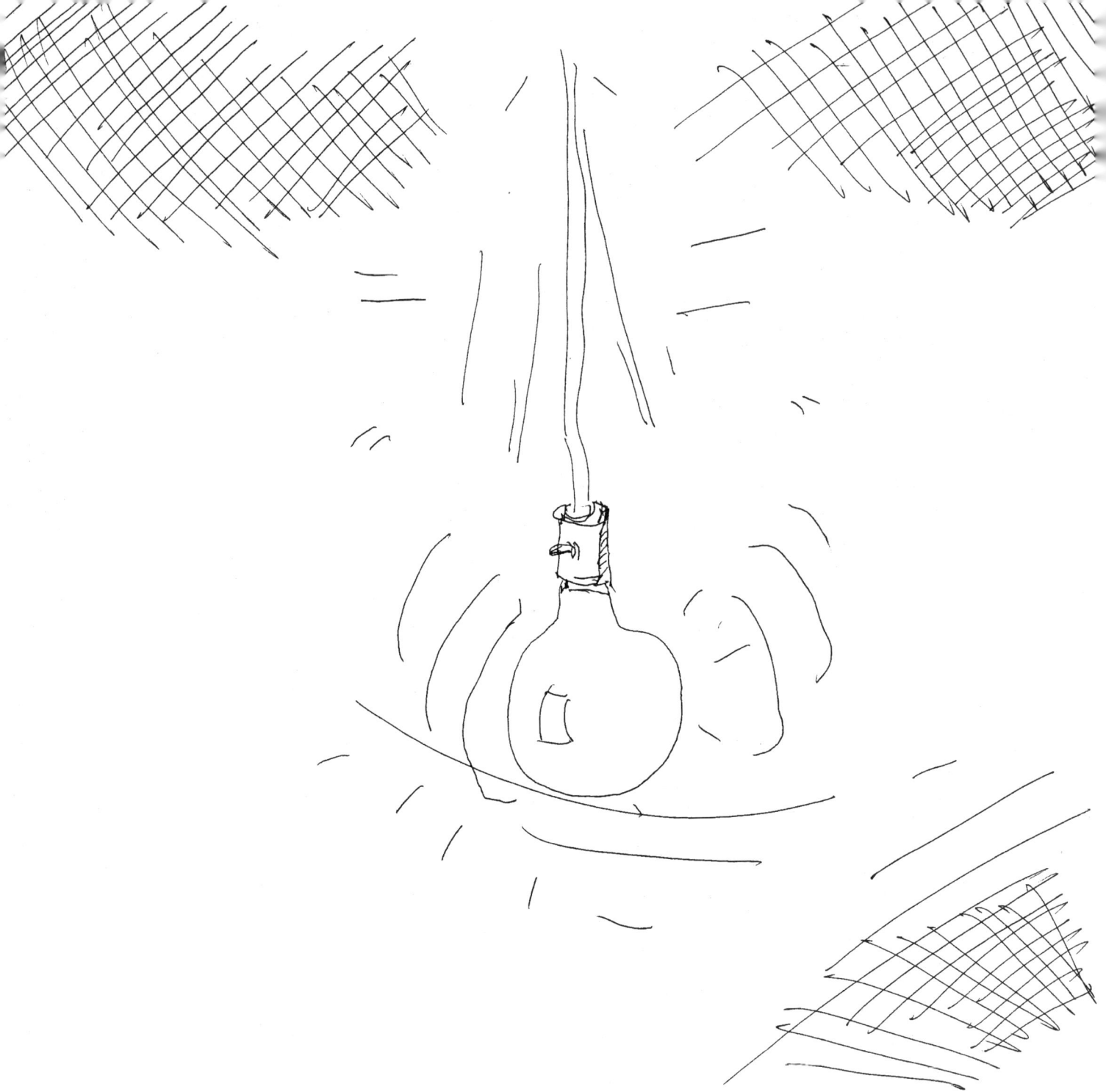

3X

THOUSANDS OF BIRDS FLOUNDERING IN STREETS

Wally Trabing

August 18, 1961, Santa Cruz

A massive flight of sooty shearwaters, fresh from a feast of anchovies, collided with shoreside structures from Pleasure Point to Rio del Mar during the night.

Residents, especially in the Pleasure Point and Capitola area were awakened about 3 a.m. today by the rain of birds, slamming against their homes.

Dead, and stunned, seabirds littered the streets and roads in the foggy, early dawn. Startled by the invasion, residents rushed out on their lawns with flashlights, then rushed back inside, as the birds flew toward their light.

Television aerial supports were severed, and one power line was shorted out about 4 a.m. on Merrill Avenue when the birds hitting the lines slapped them together.

[...] When the light of day made the area visible, residents found the streets covered with birds. The birds disgorged bits of fish and fish skeletons over the streets and lawns and housetops, leaving an overpowering fishy stench.

[...] The invasion started there yesterday afternoon, according to Joe Sunseri, owner of the Pixie Plaza Liquor store near the beach.

A sheriff's car prowling through the Pleasure Point area was rammed by several shearwaters as it shined its spotlight into the air. One bird flew full speed into a tall light standard.

Richard Von Magus, a teenager visiting on Chesterfield Drive, rushed out of a home and was struck by a bird.

227

[...] Mrs. A.E. Stadtmiller, 23007 East Cliff Drive, said she opened her front door at 6 a.m. and several of the birds tried to enter the house.

'The smell is terrible,' she said. 'The birds threw up fish all over the lawn.'

Mrs. Ethel Gudgel, 2941 Pleasure Point Drive, said she was awakened by the birds 'raining' on her roof. Many of the residents said the birds wailed and 'cried like babies' as they floundered on the ground.

[...] Harry Smith, bird bander from 1549 Escalona Drive, arrived to band 65 birds. A band from another area was discovered on one bird.

Eight persons were reported bitten by the birds.

[...] The word of the bird invasion spread fast throughout the state. Cameramen from San Francisco papers were out in the early morning fog, and a phone call came to the 'Sentinel' from Alfred Hitchcock from Hollywood, who has a home in the Santa Cruz mountains, requesting that a 'Sentinel' be sent to him.

'Santa Cruz Sentinel', Santa Cruz, 1961

The Hitchcock Castings

London

June 1 / 2, 2004
Delfina Studios
50 Bermondsey Street

Chloe Emmerson Casting

CIGAR

LIP + LIFTS HEAD

C.U.

C.U.

3½ INCH   HANDS

C.U.
CIGAR + HANDS

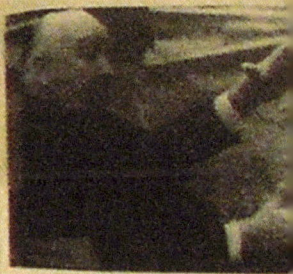

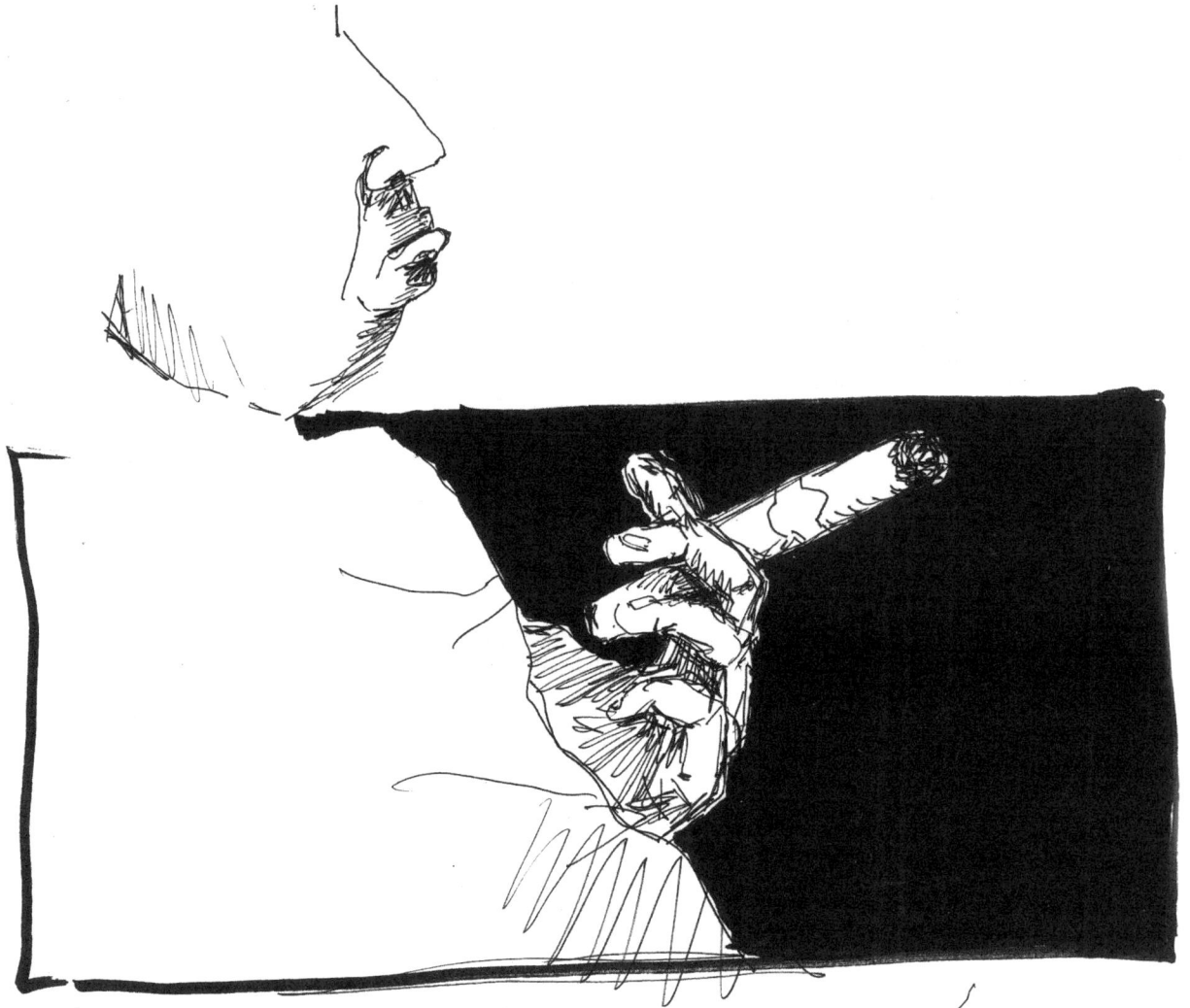

Scene   Shot   Location

Scene	Shot	Location
①	1	royal suite

1. ...H.I.T.C.H.. 3 .. (RON) / Zale & Roger
2. ...H... (Zale) ——→ walks through frame
       & Roger
3. ....
4. ....

Props
- CHANDELIER 1 METER LOWER + MOVES
- UMBRELLAS FALLING OUTSIDE (WATER SPRINKLED FOR REFL..)
- CURTAINS BY FISHING WIRE + MOVE SUBTLE
- CIGAR SMOKE FROM HITCH 3 CIGAR
- RAVEN IN CHANDELIER

Description

OVER THE SHOULDER OF SMOKING HITCH (IN PROFILE)
REVEALS UMBRELLAS FALLING OUTSIDE
...(REFLECTION FROM WATER ON UMBRELLAS)
- CURTAINS MOVE IN THE WIND
- CHANDELIER SWINGS SLIGHTLY
     + SMOKE FROM CIGAR
- Another hitch walks through the frame
         → RAVEN

Post-it notes:
- SHOOT TOWARDS NIGHT
- FRAME ONLY RED BRICK WALL

Annotations on drawing:
- Zale & Roger
- OUT OF FOCUS ??

Post-it (bottom right):
H 1 & 2
+ Hitch #4 (walking down)

Camera ...STATIC...

Lighting MAYBE SHOOT TOWARDS NIGHT
LIGHT ON UMBRELLAS
    ↳ WATER SPRINKLED ON UMBRELL..
       FOR REFLECTION

I've always wanted to be ~~someone else.~~ ?

— a woman ←

— Alfred Hitchcock P
'NONE ARE
SO BLIND

Alfred Hitchcock in *Alfred Hitchcock Presents: Episode #44: None Are So Blind*,
broadcast on October 28, 1956

JOHN BARRETT

① DAVID ALDER

② ROGER SWAINE

STEPHEN GUY DACTRY

ne **Shot** **~~ation~~**

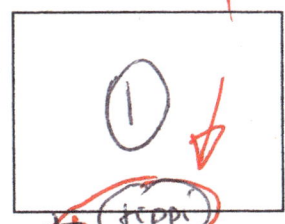
tippi is necessary

CLOSE UPS
CHRONOLOGY IN EDIT

1) H3 (RON) TURNS AROUND AS H2 (ZALE) PASSES BY
2) H2 TURNS AROUND (ZALE) = COUNTERSHOT
3) REAR-WINDOW-H (= DAD)
4) CLEANING HITCH TURNS (= JOSE) DOG
5) H4 (= film) w cello in choreography
6) RON (H3) TURNS AROUND AS H1 (= BRUCE) PASSES
— dog + tanje tippi
7) BRUCE TURNS AROUND (Towards Tippi) (= Ron + Bruce)
8) TIPPI TURNS AROUND W BIRD → WIND
9) WIND BLOWS HAT OF RON

ENCOUNTER WILL BE CLOSE TO STAIRS

+ tippi

ired
1. hitch1 = BRUCE
2. hitch2 = ZALE
3. hitch3 (RON)
4. hitch #4 w/cello
5. rear-window - hitchcock

(065 **NO CIGAR IN C.U.**
CIGAR + KRANT TO HELP

and props .....3x.. bowler hats.....
+ 3x umbrellas
— wind machine .(. + leaves.)
— cigars

Shot description ① In Close up: Hitch 3 turns his face towards the camera, as Hitch 2 passes by. ② Hitch 3 turns back towards Hitch 1, who is now approaching. ③ As Hitch 1 passes by, Hitch 3 turns his face again towards camera

Hitch1 | out of focus = BRUCE → tippi | ③ As... | ④ RON TOWARDS TIPPI

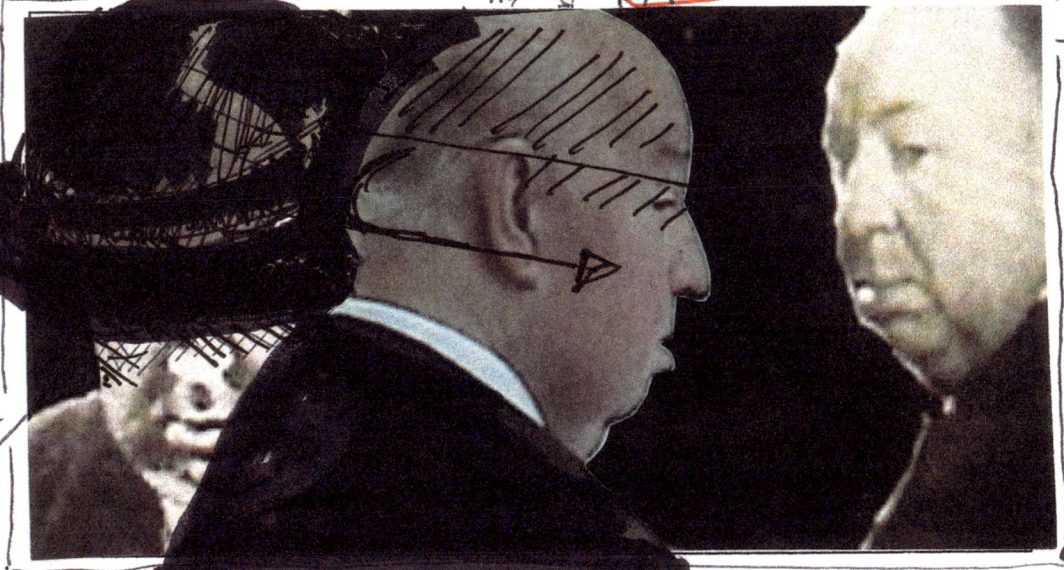

Hitch 2 = ZALE

Hitch 3 = RON 8VR

Camera .....STATIC CAMERA, CLOSE UP ON HITCH 3 (= RON)

Lighting ⓐ face of hitch 1 & 2 in shadow (or out of focus)

Ron Burrage, Hitchcock double

CLING
CLING

CLING
CLING

**Two male storks built
a nest together in a zoo
in Osnabrück, Germany,
and hatched a discarded
penguin's egg.**

Agence France-Presse, June 29, 1994, 'Fortean Times Presents:
Strange Days, The Year in Weirdness'

Roger Swaine and Erik Grimonprez, Hitchcock doubles

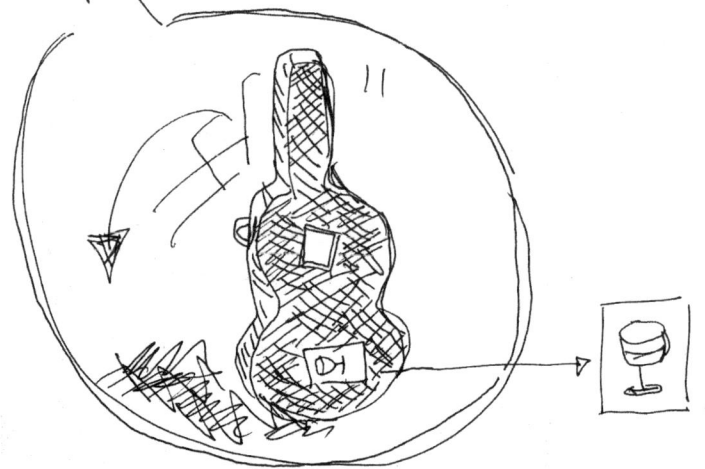

Scene   Shot   Location

| ② | ② | royal suite |

+ C.U. tippi

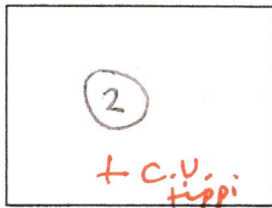

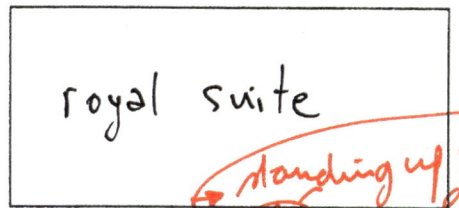

Cast required

1. (ROU) hitch #3 (sitting) Tode — standing up in dogs
2. hitch #4 w/ contrabass cello (coming in) Roger
3. hitch #2 (sitting glowing ??? ??? — cleaning hitch vacuuming leaves ???)
4. tippi ? purse + cigarette

Art direction and props

- ravens + dogs
- coffee cup on saucer + spoon + birdcage
windmachine + red leaves on floor
- cello → + extra smoke
- cigars + matches + coffee for hitch #3
- furniture suggesting cafeteria + more coffee

Shot description

① Tippi (seated) picks up her birdcage + coffee from table
(raven on her shoulder) — her purse ??
and we track her coffee cup past hitch #3 (getting up) and hitch
towards door where hitch #4 enters w/ cello who picks up his DOGS!
column?

② C.U. Tippi w/ bird on shoulder or HAND
or: just glancing ONLY EYES
SMOKES CIGARETTE
+ glancing

Roger Tode?

tippi

+ DOGS
+ RAVEN

DOG

Camera   track tippi + coffee cup

Lighting

SMOKE

CHANDELIER

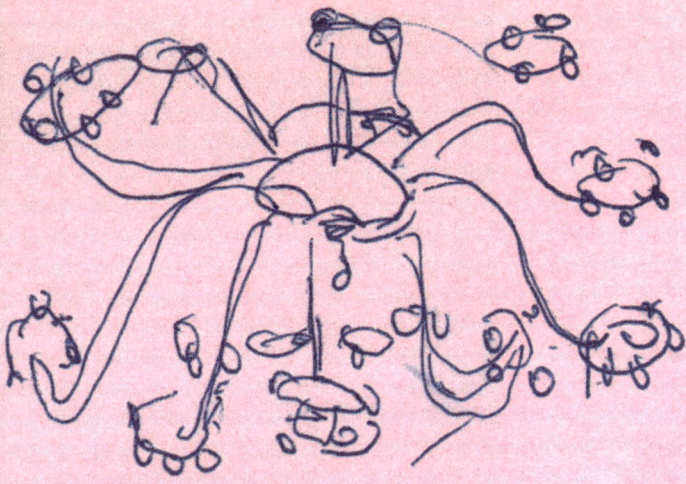
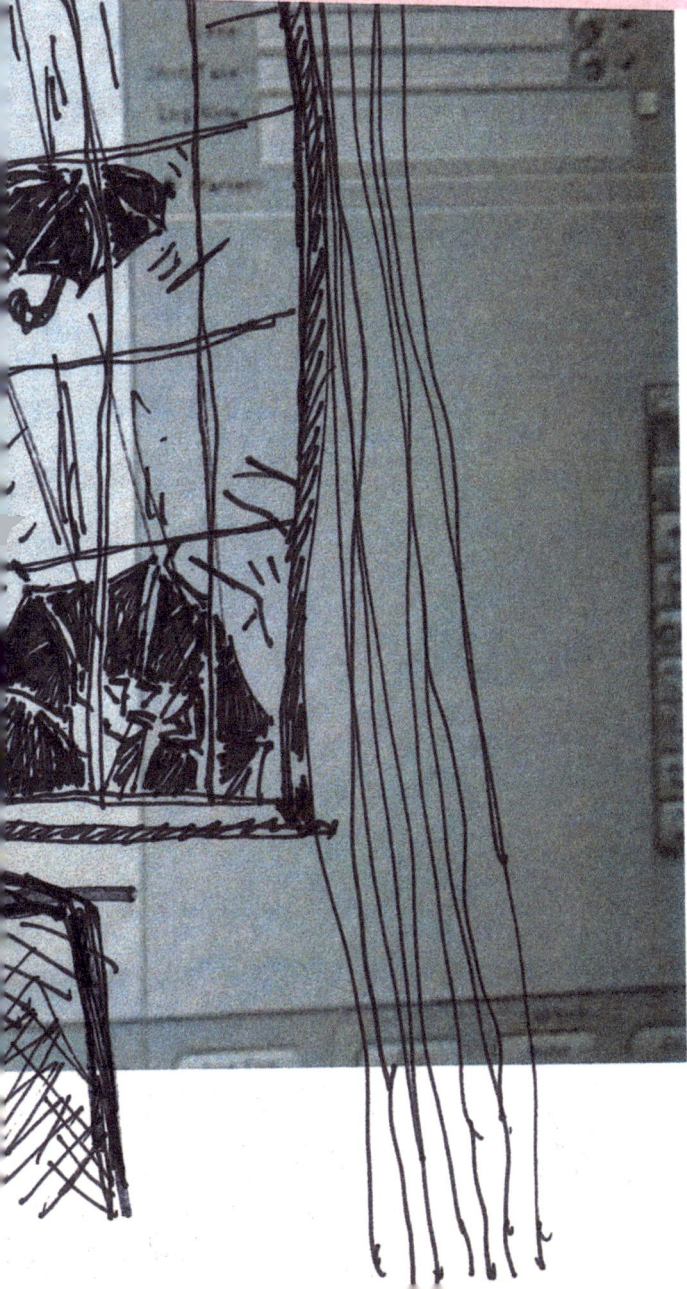

You have conquered, and I yield. Yet, henceforward art thou also dead – dead to the World, to Heaven and to Hope! In me didst thou exist – and, in my death, see by this image, which is thine own, how utterly thou hast murdered thyself.

Edgar Allen Poe, 'William Wilson'

Is there a proper way to remake a Hitchcock film?

Slavoj Žižek

'Oh, Mr. Hitchcock, in the murder scene in *Psycho*, what did you use for blood? Chicken blood?' I said, 'No, chocolate sauce.'

Alfred Hitchcock and Dr. Fredric Wertham: 'A Redbook Dialogue' in 'Hitchcock on Hitchcock', ed. Sidney Gottlieb, University of California Press, Berkeley and Los Angeles, 1995

Is there a proper way to remake a Hitchcock film?

Slavoj Žižek

Multiple Endings

There is an aspect that adds a specific density to Hitchcock's films: the implicit resonance of multiple endings. The most obvious and well-documented case is, of course, that of *Topaz*: before deciding on the ending of *Topaz* that we all know, Hitchcock shot two alternative endings, and my point is that it is not sufficient to say that he simply chose the most appropriate ending. The ending we have now rather in a way presupposes the two others, with the three endings forming a kind of syllogism, i.e. Granville (Michel Piccoli), the Russian spy, telling himself: 'They cannot prove anything about me, I can simply leave for Russia'; 'But the Russians themselves now do not want me, I am now even dangerous to them, so they will probably kill me'; 'What can I do then if in France I am outcast as a Russian spy and Russia itself no longer wants me? I can only kill myself.' There are, however, much more refined versions of this implicit presence of alternative endings. Already the denouement of Hitchcock's early melodrama *The Manxman* (1929) is preceded by two scenes which could be read as possible alternative endings (the woman kills herself; the lover never returns). Hitchcock's masterpiece *Notorious* owes at least a part of its powerful impact to the fact that its denouement should be perceived against the background of at least two other possible outcomes that resonate in it as a kind of alternative history.[1] In the first outline of the story, Alicia wins redemption by the film's end, but loses Devlin, who is killed rescuing her from the Nazis. The idea was that this sacrificial act should solve the tension between Devlin, who is unable to admit to Alicia his love for her, and Alicia, who is unable to perceive herself as worthy of love. Devlin admits his love for her without words, by dying in order to save her life. In the final scene, we find Alicia back in Miami with her group of drinking friends: although she is more 'notorious' than ever, she has in her heart the memory of a man who loved her and died for her, and, as Hitchcock put it in a memo to Selznick, 'to her this is the same as if she had achieved a life of marriage and happiness.' In the second version, the outcome is the opposite; here, we already have the idea of a slow poisoning of Alicia by Sebastian and his mother. Devlin confronts the Nazis and flees with Alicia, but Alicia dies in the process. In the epilogue, Devlin sits alone in a Rio café, where he used to meet Alicia, and overhears people discussing the death of Sebastian's

1 See the fascinating report in Thomas Schatz, 'The Genius of the System', New York, Hold and Co. (1996), p. 393–403.

wanton and treacherous wife. However, the letter in his hands is a commendation from President Truman citing Alicia's bravery. Devlin pockets the letter and finishes his drink. Finally, the version we know was arrived at, together with a finale that implies that Devlin and Alicia are now married. Hitchcock then left this finale out, to end on a more tragic note, with Sebastian, who truly loved Alicia, left to face the Nazis' deadly wrath. The point is that both alternative endings (Devlin's and Alicia's death) are incorporated into the film, as a kind of fantasmatic background of the action we see on the screen: if they are to constitute a couple, both Devlin and Alicia have to undergo a 'symbolic death', so that the happy ending emerges from the combination of two unhappy endings, i.e. these two alternative fantasmatic scenarios sustain the denouement we actually see.

This feature allows us to insert Hitchcock in the series of artists whose work forecast today's digital universe. Art historians have often noted the phenomenon of the old artistic forms pushing against their own boundaries and using procedures which, at least from our retroactive view, seem to point towards a new technology that will be able to serve as a more 'natural' and appropriate 'objective correlative' to the life-experience the old forms endeavoured to render by means of their 'excessive' experimentation. A whole series of narrative procedures in nineteenth-century novels announce not only the standard narrative cinema (the intricate use of 'flashback' in Emily Brontë or of 'cross-cutting' and 'close-ups' in Dickens), but sometimes even the modernist cinema (the use of 'off-space' in 'Madame Bovary'), as if a new perception of life was already here, but was still struggling to find its proper means of articulation, until it finally found it in cinema. What we have here is thus the historicity of a kind of *futur antérieur*: it is only when cinema was here and developed its standard procedures that we can really grasp the narrative logic of Dickens's great novels or Flaubert's 'Madame Bovary'.

And is it not the case that today we are approaching a homologous threshold? A new 'life experience' is in the air, a perception of life that explodes the form of the linear-centred narrative and renders life as a multiform flow even in the domain of 'hard' sciences (quantum physics and its multiple reality interpretation, or the utter contingency that provides the spin to the actual evolution of the life on Earth – as Stephen Jay Gould demonstrates in his 'Wonderful Life', the fossils of Burgess Shale bear witness to how evolution may have taken a wholly different turn[2]). We seem to be haunted by the chanciness of life and the alternate versions of reality. Either life is experienced as a series of multiple parallel destinies that interact and are crucially affected by meaningless contingent encounters, the point at which one series intersects with and

2 See Stephen Jay Gould, 'Wonderful Life', New York, Norton (1989).

intervenes into another (see Altman's *Short Cuts*), or different versions/outcomes of the same plot are repeatedly enacted (the 'parallel universes' or 'alternative possible worlds' scenarios – see Kieslowski's *Blind Chance, The Double Life of Veronique* and *Red*. Even 'serious' historians recently produced a volume 'Virtual History', that reads the major events of the Modern Age, from Cromwell's victory over the Stuarts and the American War of Independence to the disintegration of Communism, as hinging on unpredictable and sometimes even improbable chances[3].) This perception of our reality as one of the possible – often even not the most probable – outcomes of an 'open' situation, this notion that other possible outcomes are not simply cancelled out but continue to haunt our 'true' reality as a spectre of what might have happened, conferring on our reality the status of extreme fragility and contingency, implicitly clashes with the predominant 'linear' narrative forms of our literature and cinema. They seem to call for a new artistic medium in which they would not be an eccentric excess, but its 'proper' mode of functioning. The notion of creation also changes with this new experience of the world: it no longer designates the positive act of imposing a new order, but rather the *negative* gesture of choice, of limiting the possibilities, of privileging one option at the expense of all the others. One can argue that the cyberspace hypertext *is* this new medium in which this life experience will find its 'natural', more appropriate, objective correlative, so that, again, it is only with the advent of cyberspace hypertext that we can effectively grasp what Altman and Kieslowski – and, implicitly, also Hitchcock – were effectively aiming at.

THE IDEAL REMAKE

These reflections, perhaps, also suggest what a proper remake of a Hitchcock film would be. To try and imitate Hitchcockian sinthoms is an exercise in advance condemned to failure; to remake the same narrative results in a 'Shakespeare Made Easy' output. So there are only two ways left. One is indicated by Gus van Sant's *Psycho* which, paradoxically, I am inclined to consider a failed masterpiece, rather than a simple failure. The idea of an exact frame-by-frame remake is an ingenious idea, and, in my view, the problem is that the film did not go far enough in this direction. Ideally, what the film should strive for is to achieve the uncanny effect of the double: in shooting formally the same film, the difference would have became all the more palpable – everything would have been the same – shots, angles, dialogue – and, nonetheless, on account of this very sameness, we would all the more powerfully experience that we are dealing with a totally different film. This gap would have been signalled by barely perceptible nuances in the way of acting, in the choice of actors, in the use

3 See 'Virtual History', edited by Niall Ferguson, London, MacMillan 1997.

of colour, etc. Some elements in van Sant's film already point in this direction: the roles of Norman, Lilah (portrayed as a lesbian) and Marion (a non-maternal, withdrawn, cold bitch in contrast to the big-breasted maternal Janet Leigh), even Arbogast and Sam, nicely indicate the shift from late fifties to today's universe. While some added shots (such as the enigmatic subjective shots of a cloudy sky during the two murders) are also acceptable, problems resurface with the more brutal changes (like Norman's masturbation while he peeps on Marion before slaughtering her – one is tempted to make the rather obvious point that, in this case, i.e. if he were to be able to arrive at this kind of sexual satisfaction, there would have been no need for him to accomplish the violent *passage à l'acte* and slaughter Marion!); to top it all, some scenes are completely ruined, their impact is completely lost, by a change to Hitchcock's precise framing (for example, the key scene in which, after leaving her office with the money, Marion at home prepares to escape). Hitchcock's own remakes (the two versions of *The Man Who Knew Too Much*, as well as *Saboteur* and *North by Northwest*) point in this direction: although the narrative is very similar, the underlying libidinal economy is wholly different in each of the subsequent remakes, as if the sameness serves the purpose of marking the Difference.[4]

The second way would be to stage, in a well-calculated strategic move, one of the alternative scenarios that underlie those actualised by Hitchcock, like the remake of *Notorious* with Ingrid Bergman surviving alone. This would be a proper way to honour Hitchcock as the artist that belongs to our era. Perhaps, more than de Palma's and others' direct 'hommages' to Hitchcock, the scenes that announce such a proper remake are to be found in unexpected places, like the scene in the hotel room, the place of crime, in Francis Ford Coppola's *The Conversation*: Coppola is certainly not a Hitchcockian, yet the investigator inspects the room with a Hitchcockian gaze, like Lila and Sam do with Marion's motel room, moving from the main bedroom to the bathroom and focusing there on the toilet and the shower. The shift from the shower (where there are no traces of the crime, where everything is clean) to the toilet sink, elevating it into the Hitchcockian object that attracts our gaze, fascinating us with its premonitions of some unspeakable horror, is crucial here (recall Hitchcock's battle with censorship to allow the inside view of the toilet, from where Lila picks up a torn piece of paper with Marion's writing on it, the proof that she was there). After a series of obvious references to *Psycho* apropos of the shower (quickly pulling open the curtain, inspecting the hole in the sink), the investigator focuses on the (allegedly cleansed) toilet seat, flushes it, and then the stain appears as if out of nowhere, blood and other traces of the crime overflowing the edge of the sink. This scene, a kind of *Psycho* reread through *Marnie* (with

4 Perhaps the greatest achievement of van Sant's remake is the scene of final credits, which follows the shot that ends Hitchcock's film and goes on for several minutes. A continuous crane shot showing what goes on around the car being dragged out of the swamp, the bored policemen around the towing truck, all this accompanied with a soft guitar repeating in an improvised way the main motif of Herrmann's score, this feature supplements the film with the unique touch of the Nineties.

its red stain blurring the screen) contains the main elements of the Hitchcockian universe: it has the Hitchcockian object which materialises some unspecified threat, functioning as the hole into another abyssal dimension (is flushing the toilet in this scene not like pushing the wrong button that dissolves the entire universe in science-fiction novels?). This object that simultaneously attracts and repels the subject can be said to be the point from which the inspected setting returns the gaze (is it not that the hero is somehow regarded by the toilet sink?). Coppola realises the alternative scenario of the toilet itself as the ultimate locus of mystery. What makes this mini-remake of a scene so effective is that Coppola suspends the prohibition operative in *Psycho*: the threat *does* explode, the camera *does* show the danger hanging in the air in *Psycho*, the chaotic bloody mess erupting from the toilet. Furthermore, is not the swamp behind the house in which Norman drowns the cars with the bodies of his victims a kind of gigantic pool of excremental mud, so that one can say that he in a way flushes the cars down the toilet – the famous moment of the worried expression on his face when Marion's car stops its immersion into the swamp for a couple of seconds effectively signals the worry that the toilet did not swallow the traces of our 'crime'? The very last shot of *Psycho*, in which we see Marion's car being pulled out of the swamp, is thus a kind of Hitchcockian equivalent to the blood re-emerging from the toilet sink – in short, this swamp is another in the series of the entrance-points to the pre-ontological Netherworld.

And is not the same reference to the pre-ontological Underworld operative also in the final scene of *Vertigo*? In pre-digital times, when I was in my teens, I remember seeing a bad copy of *Vertigo* – its last seconds were missing, so that the movie appeared to have a happy ending: Scottie reconciled with Judy, forgiving her and accepting her as a partner, the two of them passionately embracing. My point is that such an ending is not as artificial as it may seem: it is rather in the actual ending that the sudden appearance of the Mother Superior from the staircase below functions as a kind of negative *deus ex machina*, a sudden intrusion in no way properly grounded in the narrative logic, which prevents the happy ending.[5] Where does the nun come from? From the same pre-ontological realm of shadows from which Scottie himself secretly observes Madeleine in the florist's.[6] It is the reference to this pre-ontological realm that allows us to approach the quintessential Hitchcockian scene which was never shot – precisely because it renders the basic matrix of his work directly, its actual filming undoubtedly would have produced a vulgar, tasteless effect. Here is this scene that Hitchcock wanted to insert in *North by Northwest*, as reported in Truffaut's conversations with the Master:

5 Is this sudden appearance not similar to Wagner's *Tristan*? Towards the very end of the opera, after Tristan's death, Isolde's arrival and plunging into the death trance, the break occurs with the arrival of another, second, ship, when the slow progress all of a sudden accelerates in an almost comic way – in five minutes more events happen than in all the previous opera (there is a fight, Melot and Kurwenal die, ...) – similar to Verdi's *Il Trovatore*, where in the last two minutes a whole package of things happen. Such unexpected intrusions just before the ending are crucial for the reading of the underlying tensions of a narrative.

6 When Lesley Brill claims that in *Under Capricorn* is a kind of underworld creature trying to drag Ingrid Bergman back into hell, one is tempted to say that the nun which appears at the very end of *Vertigo* belongs to the same evil netherworld – the paradox being, of course, that she is a *nun*, a woman of God, who embodies the force of Evil that drags the subject down and prevents her salvation.

I wanted to have a long dialogue between Cary Grant and one of the factory workers [at a Ford automobile plant] as they walk along the assembly line. Behind them a car is being assembled, piece by piece. Finally, the car they've seen being put together from a simple nut and bolt is complete, with gas and oil, and all ready to drive off the line. The two men look at each other and say, 'Isn't it wonderful!' Then they open the door of the car and out drops a corpse.[7]

Where did this corpse emerge, or fall, from? Again, from the very void from which Scottie observes Madeleine in the florist's – or, from the void from which blood emerges in *The Conversation*. (One should also bear in mind that what we would have seen in this long shot is the elementary unity of the production process – is then the corpse that mysteriously drops out from nowhere not the perfect stand-in for the surplus value that is generated 'out of nowhere' through the production process?)

This shocking elevation of the ridiculously lowest (the Beyond where shit disappears) into the metaphysical Sublime is perhaps one of the mysteries of Hitchcock's art. Is not the Sublime sometimes part of our most common everyday experience? When, in the midst of accomplishing a simple task (say, climbing the long line of stairs), we are overwhelmed by an unexpected fatigue, it all of a sudden appears as if the simple goal we want to reach (the top of the stairs) is separated from us by an unfathomable barrier and thus changed into a metaphysical Object forever out of our reach, as if there is something which forever prevents us from accomplishing it. And the domain where excrement vanishes after we flush the toilet is effectively one of the metaphors for the horrifying Sublime, beyond of the primordial, pre-ontological Chaos into which things disappear. Although we rationally know what happens to our excrement, the imaginary mystery nonetheless persists – shit remains an excess which does not fit our daily reality, and Lacan was right in claiming that we pass from animals to humans the moment an animal has problems with what to do with its excrement, the moment it turns into an excess that annoys it.[8] The Real in the scene from *The Conversation* is thus not primarily the horrifyingly disgusting stuff re-emerging from the toilet sink, but rather the hole itself, the gap which serves as the passage to a different ontological order. The similarity between the empty toilet sink before the remainders of the murder re-emerge from it and Malevich's *Black Square on White Surface* is significant here: does the look from above into the toilet sink not reproduce almost the same 'minimalist' visual scheme, a black (or, at least, darker) square of water enframed by the white surface of the sink itself? Again we, of course, know that the excrements

7 Francois Truffaut, 'Hitchcock', New York: Simon and Schuster (1985), p. 257.

8 It's similar with saliva: as we all know, although we can without problem swallow our own saliva, we find it extremely repulsive to swallow again a saliva which was spat out of our body – again a case of violating the Inside/Outside frontier.

which disappear are somewhere in the sewage network – what is 'real' here is the topological hole or torsion which 'curves' the space of our reality so that we perceive/imagine excrement as disappearing into an alternative dimension which is not part of our everyday reality.

Hitchcock's obsession with a spotless bathroom is well known,[9] and it is significant that, when, after Marion's murder, he wants to shift our point of identification to Norman, he does this with a long rendering of the careful process of cleansing the bathroom. This is perhaps the key scene of the film, a scene that provides an uncannily profound satisfaction of a job properly done, of things returning back to normal, of a situation again under control, of the traces of the horrifying netherworld being erased. One is tempted to read this scene against the background of the well-known proposition of Saint Thomas of Aquinas according to which a virtue (defined as a proper way to accomplish an act) can also serve evil purposes: one can also be a perfect thief, murderer, extortioner, i.e. accomplish an evil act in a 'virtuous' way. What this scene of cleansing the bathroom in *Psycho* demonstrates is how the 'lower' perfection can imperceptibly affect the 'higher' goal: Norman's virtuous perfection in cleansing the bathroom, of course, serves the evil purpose of erasing the traces of the crime; however, this very perfection, the dedication and the thoroughness of his act, seduces us, the spectators, into assuming that, if someone acts in such a 'perfect' way, he should be in his entirety a good and sympathetic person. In short, someone who cleanses the bathroom so thoroughly as Norman does cannot be really bad, in spite of his other minor peculiarities... (Or, to put it even more pointedly, in a country governed by Norman, trains would certainly run on time!) While watching this scene recently, I caught myself nervously noticing that the bathroom was not properly cleansed – two small stains on the side of the bathtub remained! I almost wanted to shout: hey, it's not yet over, finish the job properly!

THE ENDINGS OF *PSYCHO*

I never found convincing the standard explanation of the Leftist theorists who cannot help but to love Hitchcock: yes, his universe is male chauvinist, but at the same time he renders visible its cracks and as it were subverts it from within. I think the social-political dimension of Hitchcock's films is to be sought elsewhere.

Let us take the two closures at the end of *Psycho* – first the psychiatrist wraps up the story, then Norman/Mother delivers the final monologue of 'I wouldn't even hurt a fly!' This split between the two closures tells us more about the deadlocks of contemporary subjectivity than a dozen essays in

9 He liked to boast that after he left the toilet, no one could, upon inspecting it, guess that someone had been in there using it.

Usually I play a passer-by, but you can't have a passer-by out on the ocean… I hit on a good idea. At the time, I was on a strenuous diet, painfully working my way from 300 to 200 pounds. So I decided to immortalise my loss and get my bit part by posing for 'before' and 'after' pictures in a newspaper ad.

Alfred Hitchcock in François Truffaut, 'Hitchcock Interviews', Touchstone Edition, Simon & Schuster, New York, 1983

cultural criticism. That is to say, it may appear that we are dealing with the well-known split between expert knowledge and our private solipsistic universe, deplored by many social critics today: common sense, a shared set of ethically engaged presuppositions, is slowly disintegrating, and what we get are two points of view. On the one hand, the objectivised language of experts and scientists which can no longer be translated into the common language accessible to everyone, but which is present in it nonetheless in the mode of fetishised formulas that no one really understands yet which shape our artistic and popular imaginary (Black Hole, Big Bang, Superstrings, Quantum Oscillation...). On the other hand, the multitude of lifestyles that fail to commune with one another so that all we can do is secure the conditions for their tolerant coexistence in a multicultural society. The icon of today's subject is perhaps the proverbial Indian computer programmer who during the day excels in his expertise, while in the evening, upon returning home, lights a candle to the local Hindu divinity and respects the sacredness of the cow.

However, upon closer look, it soon becomes apparent how this opposition is displaced at the end of *Psycho*. It is the psychiatrist, the representative of cold objective knowledge, who speaks in an engaged, almost warmly human way, his explanation full of personal tics and sympathetic gestures. Norman, withdrawn into his private world, is precisely no longer himself, but totally possessed by another psychic entity, the mother's ghost. This final image of Norman reminds me of the way they shoot soap operas in Mexico: because of the extremely tight schedule (the studio has to produce each day a half-hour instalment of the series), actors do not have time to learn their lines in advance, so they simply have hidden in their ears a tiny voice receiver, and a man the cabin behind the set simply reads to them the instructions on what they are to do (what words they are to say, what acts they are to accomplish, etc.) Actors are trained to react immediately, with no delay, to these instructions. This is Norman at the end of *Psycho*, and this is also a good lesson to those New Age types who claim that we should drop the social masks and set free our innermost true selves. Well, we see the final result in Norman who, at the end of *Psycho*, effectively realizes his true Self and follows the old Rimbaud motto from his letter to Demeny ('Car je est un autre. Si le cuivre s'éveille clairon, il n'y a rien de sa faute'[10]): If Norman starts to talk with the strange voice of his mother, it's none of his guilt. The price I have to pay in order to become 'really myself', the undivided subject, is total alienation, becoming an Other with regard to myself: the obstacle to my full self-identity is the very condition of my Selfhood.

Another aspect of this same antagonism concerns architecture: one can also consider Norman as the subject split between the two houses, the modern

10 'I is an Other. If the bugle is woken by the brass, it's not its fault.'

horizontal motel and the vertical Gothic mother's house, forever running between the two, never finding a proper place of his own. In this sense, the *unheimlich* character of the film's end means that, in his full identification with the mother, he finally found his *heim*, his home. In modernist works such as *Psycho*, this split is still visible, while the main goal of today's post-modern architecture is to obfuscate it. Suffice it to recall the 'New Urbanism' with its return to small family houses in small towns, with front porches, recreating the cosy atmosphere of the local community – clearly, this is the case of architecture as ideology at its purest, providing an imaginary (albeit 'real,' materialised in the actual disposition of houses) solution to a social deadlock which has nothing to do with architecture and all to do with late capitalist dynamics. A more ambiguous case of the same antagonism is the work of Frank Gehry: why is he so popular, a true cult figure? He takes as the basis one of the two poles of the antagonism, either the old-fashioned family house or a modernist concrete-and-glass building, and then either submits it to a kind of cubist anamorphic distortion (curved angles of walls and windows, etc.) or combines the old family home with a modernist supplement, in which case, as Fredric Jameson pointed out, the focal point is the place (the room) at the intersection of the two spaces. In short, is Gehry not doing in architecture what the Caduveo Indians (in Lévi-Strauss' magnificent description from his 'Tristes Tropiques') were trying to achieve with their tattooed faces: to resolve through a symbolic act the real of a social antagonism by constructing a utopian solution, a mediation between the opposites? So here is my final thesis: if the Bates Motel were to be built by Gehry, directly combining the old mother's house and the flat modern motel into a new hybrid entity, there would have been no need for Norman to kill his victims, since he would have been relieved of the unbearable tension that compels him to run between the two places – he would have a third place of mediation between the two extremes.

Excerpt from 'Is there a proper way to remake a Hitchcock film?', reproduced by kind permission of the author.

Trailer for *The Birds*

Since we were unable to finish the story last time, we should have another stab at it tonight.

Alfred Hitchcock in *Alfred Hitchcock Presents: Episode #65: I Killed The Count (Part II)*, broadcast on March 24, 1957

Dead Birds Rain Down on Towns Half a World Apart

Three weeks ago, thousands of crows, pigeons, wattles and honeyeaters fell out of the sky in Esperance, Western Australia. Then last week dozens of grackles, sparrows and pigeons dropped dead on two streets in Austin, Texas.

Richard Shears
http://www.dailymail.co.uk
Last updated at 22:00pm on 10th January 2007

Possibly, you could say that one evening, late in the future, all the mirrors in the world decided to join together. Whilst most people would consider mirrors merely as reflective surfaces, some of the more mystical religions proposed them to be doors, into some other, deeper realm. Rather now, see them as veins; the veins of some vast hidden creature along which light can travel. A creature with blood photons.

For centuries this creature knotted its veins together, in such a way that each journey of light came back to its starting point. Thus, we saw ourselves. But now, with this joining at the silver, each mirror reflected not the astonished gaze of the owner, but the equally shocked expression of another, stranger face. A stranger's face.

At which you could only grimace, or bellow, or stand dumbfounded in front of.

We have to imagine the mirror creature shrugging itself, perhaps, and coming out of the shrug with its tangle of veins rearranged into a new pattern. Perhaps it didn't mean this to happen. Perhaps it did.

Destroying the mirrors brought no respite, for each replacement mirror bought, or indeed created, would still reflect the same stranger's image. Also, it was quickly noted, no matter where in the world the viewer was, no matter through which foreign mirror he or she gazed, the same partner would always be waiting there.

This phenomenon became known as the Silvering. In time, the imagined monster through which the rays of light ran was called by the same name.

The exact mathematical shape that the Silvering's veins would have to follow, for the process to take place, was discovered to be a highly complex eleventh-dimensional curve. The abstract beauty of this curve may have pleased the scientists; but it was of little use to all the billions of people in the world who now found their mirrors completely useless for their given task. To take a most obvious example: how could some young woman with long tresses of flowing hair possibly groom herself in the reflected image of some old, decrepit bald man?

For yes, some men were reflected by women. The Silvering knew no prejudice. The old were mirrored by the young; gays by straights; blacks by whites; the rich by the poor. At first this dissolving of boundaries brought only anger on both sides of the glass. Fortunately, although light waves would travel through the Silvering's veins, sound waves could not. Curses were not heard, but, of course, easily imagined from the expressions on a face.

But then, and only after a very short time, the people of the world came to accept their new reflections, and to work with them. And thus it was that old, decrepit bald men learned how to mime the combing of long golden tresses. And the world was considered a better place for the joining at the silver.

The only distressing moments came about because of a simple mathematical property: each of the Silvering's veins had only two points of entry – a beginning and an end. Because of this, the process only worked when the number of people in the world was an even number. Given the eternal play of birth and death, every so often a person would go to their mirror, expecting their partner to greet them, only to find themselves staring at a blank space, an emptiness, a terrifying void.

This phenomenon was known as the Clouding, and brought about an avoidance of all mirrors, until such day as the global population turned back from odd, to even, and all the veins of light had both beginnings, and endings.

A new face would appear to embrace your reflection, and the smiles were perfectly copied. Making balance in the world.

Until the Silvering shrugged once more; not only through space, but through the past and the future as well. So that possibly one day, late in the evening, you could say that all the mirrors of all time...

Jeff Noon, 'The Silvering'
from his collection 'Pixel Juice', Transworld 1998

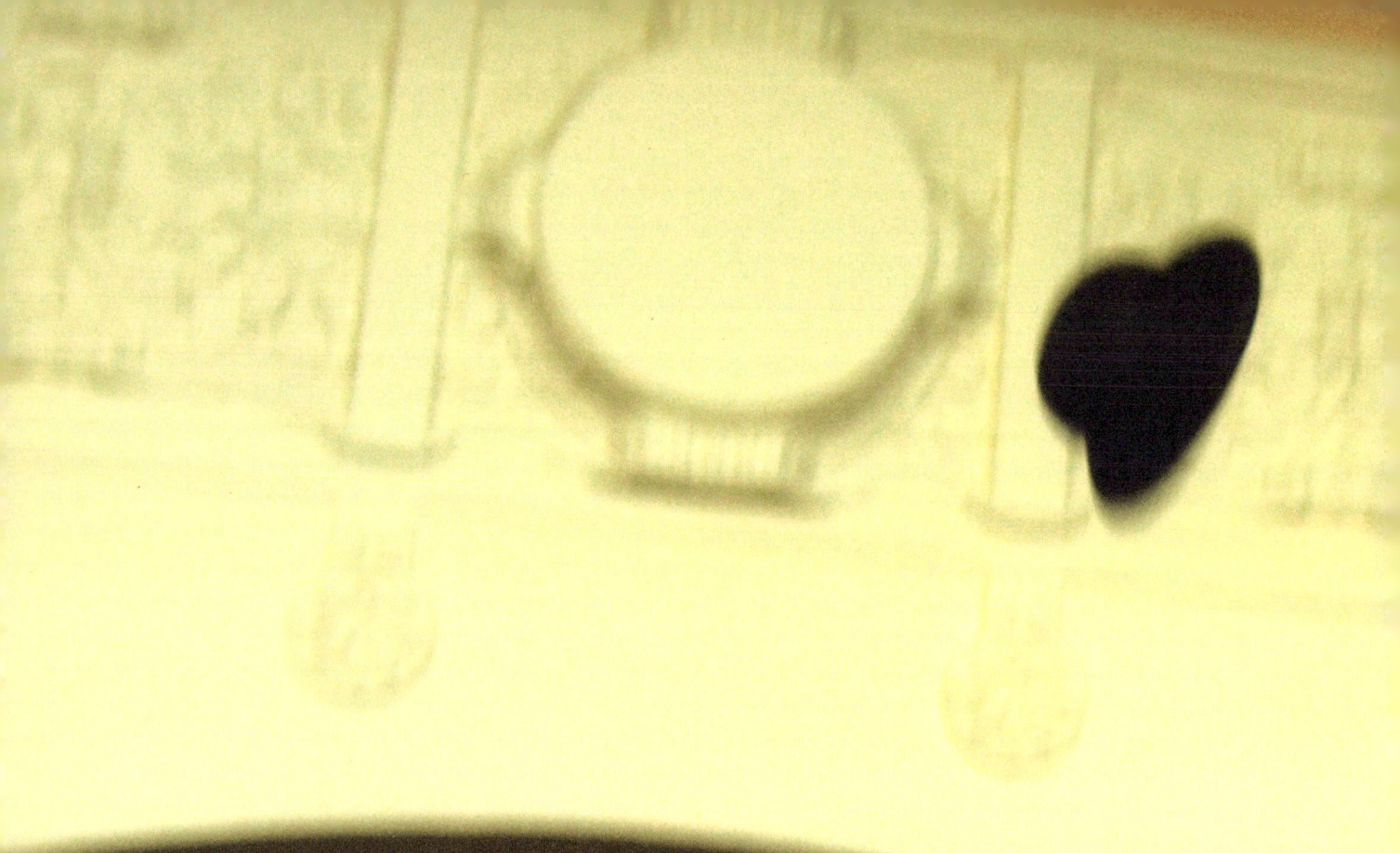

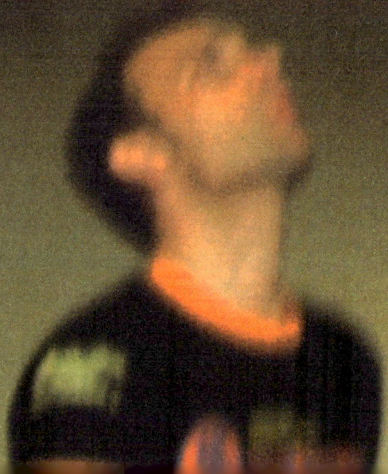

PHOTOCREDITS

p4-5 Photography Theo Volpatti, © Theo Volpatti & Johan Grimonprez

p6-7 Sketches © Johan Grimonprez

p8-9 Drawings © Johan Grimonprez

p16-7 Drawings © Johan Grimonprez

p18-9 Photography Theo Volpatti, © Theo Volpatti & Johan Grimonprez

p22-3 Photography Theo Volpatti, © Theo Volpatti & Johan Grimonprez

p28-9 Photography Theo Volpatti, © Theo Volpatti & Johan Grimonprez

p34-5 Sketches © Johan Grimonprez

p38-9 Photography Theo Volpatti, © Theo Volpatti & Johan Grimonprez

p40-1 Ron Burrage, casting material for *Looking for Alfred* as featured in *Double Take* © Johan Grimonprez

p42-3 Digital collage © Johan Grimonprez, digital imaging by Kristien Daem

p46-7 Photography Theo Volpatti, © Theo Volpatti & Johan Grimonprez

p48-9 Ron Burrage, Photography Theo Volpatti, © Theo Volpatti & Johan Grimonprez

p50-1 Drawings © Johan Grimonprez

p52-3 Photography Theo Volpatti, © Theo Volpatti & Johan Grimonprez

p60-1 Film still from *Looking for Alfred* © Johan Grimonprez, digital imaging by Kristien Daem

p68-9 Drawings © Johan Grimonprez

p72-3 Photography Theo Volpatti, © Theo Volpatti & Johan Grimonprez

p74-5 Digital collage © Johan Grimonprez, digital imaging by Kristien Daem

p82 Erik Grimonprez, photography Theo Volpatti, © Theo Volpatti & Johan Grimonprez

p85 Erik Grimonprez, photography Theo Volpatti, © Theo Volpatti & Johan Grimonprez

p90-1 Photography Theo Volpatti, © Theo Volpatti & Johan Grimonprez

p92-3 Still from *Double Take* © Johan Grimonprez

p94-5 Digital collage © Johan Grimonprez, with film still from *The Birds* © 1963 Alfred J. Hitchcock Productions, Inc., courtesy of Universal Studios Licensing LLLP

p100-1 Digital collage © Johan Grimonprez, with film still from *The Birds* © 1963 Alfred J. Hitchcock Productions, Inc., courtesy of Universal Studios Licensing LLLP

p106-7 Photography Theo Volpatti, © Theo Volpatti & Johan Grimonprez

p108-9 Sketches © Johan Grimonprez

p110-1 Digital collage © Johan Grimonprez, incorporating publicity still from *The Birds* © Corbis

p112-3 Photography Theo Volpatti, © Theo Volpatti & Johan Grimonprez

p114-5 Sketches © Johan Grimonprez

p116-7 Photography Theo Volpatti, © Theo Volpatti & Johan Grimonprez

p118-9 Photography Theo Volpatti, © Theo Volpatti & Johan Grimonprez

p120-1 Collages © Johan Grimonprez

p122-3 Photography Theo Volpatti, © Theo Volpatti & Johan Grimonprez

p124-5 Photography Mathias Kessler, © Johan Grimonprez

p126-7 Photography Theo Volpatti, © Theo Volpatti & Johan Grimonprez

p128-9 Sketches © Johan Grimonprez

p130-1 Photography Mathias Kessler, © Johan Grimonprez

p132 Sketches © Johan Grimonprez

p133 Photography Mathias Kessler, © Johan Grimonprez

p134-5 Photography Mathias Kessler, © Johan Grimonprez

p144-5 Still from *The Alfred Hitchcock Hour* as featured in *Double Take* © Johan Grimonprez

p150-1 Sketches © Johan Grimonprez

p152-3 Photography Theo Volpatti, © Theo Volpatti & Johan Grimonprez

p158-9 Film still from *Looking for Alfred* © Johan Grimonprez, digital imaging by Kristien Daem

p162-3 Photography Theo Volpatti, © Theo Volpatti & Johan Grimonprez

p170-71 Photography Daragh Reeves, © Johan Grimonprez

p172-3 Photography Theo Volpatti, © Theo Volpatti & Johan Grimonprez

p174-5 Sketches © Johan Grimonprez

p176-7 Photography Theo Volpatti, © Theo Volpatti & Johan Grimonprez

p178-9 Sketches © Johan Grimonprez, with photography © Theo Volpatti

p180-1 Photography Theo Volpatti, © Theo Volpatti & Johan Grimonprez

p182-3 Photography Theo Volpatti, © Theo Volpatti & Johan Grimonprez

p184-5 Sketches © Johan Grimonprez

p186-7 Film still from *The Birds* © 1963 Alfred J. Hitchcock Productions, Inc., courtesy of Universal Studios Licensing LLLP

p188-9 Film still from *Double Take,* © Johan Grimonprez, digital imaging by Kristien Daem

p190-1 Sketches © Johan Grimonprez

p192-3 Photography © Kristien Daem & Johan Grimonprez

p194-5 Film still from *Looking for Alfred* © Johan Grimonprez, digital imaging by Kristien Daem

p196-7 Photography Theo Volpatti, © Theo Volpatti & Johan Grimonprez

p200-1 Sketches © Johan Grimonprez

p202-3 Photography Theo Volpatti, © Theo Volpatti & Johan Grimonprez

p204-5 Photography Theo Volpatti, © Theo Volpatti & Johan Grimonprez

p210 René Magritte: *La Reproduction interdite* (Not to be Reproduced), 1937 © ADAGP, Paris and DACS, London 2007

p214-5 Digital collage © Johan Grimonprez, with film still from *The Birds* © 1963 Alfred J. Hitchcock Productions, Inc., courtesy of Universal Studios Licensing LLLP

p218-9 Film still from *Looking for Alfred* © Johan Grimonprez, digital imaging by Kristien Daem

p220 Photography Theo Volpatti, © Theo Volpatti & Johan Grimonprez

p224-5 Sketches © Johan Grimonprez

p230-1 Photography Theo Volpatti, © Theo Volpatti & Johan Grimonprez

p232-3 Sketches © Johan Grimonprez

p234-5 Sketches © Johan Grimonprez Photography Theo Volpatti, © Theo Volpatti & Johan Grimonprez

p236-7 Sketches © Johan Grimonprez

p238-9 Photography Theo Volpatti, © Theo Volpatti & Johan Grimonprez

p240-1 Photography Theo Volpatti, © Theo Volpatti & Johan Grimonprez

p242-3 Sketches © Johan Grimonprez

p244-5 Photography Theo Volpatti, © Theo Volpatti & Johan Grimonprez

p246-7 Sketches © Johan Grimonprez

p248-9 Photography Theo Volpatti, © Theo Volpatti & Johan Grimonprez

p250-1 Sketches © Johan Grimonprez

p252-3 Sketches © Johan Grimonprez

p254-5 Photography Theo Volpatti © Theo Volpatti & Johan Grimonprez

p256-7 Film still from the shoot of *Looking for Alfred* as featured in *Double Take* © Johan Grimonprez, digital imaging by Kristien Daem

p266-7 Photography Theo Volpatti, © Theo Volpatti & Johan Grimonprez

p270-1 Film still from *Lifeboat* © 1944 Twentieth Century Fox. All rights reserved

p274-5 Digital collage © Johan Grimonprez, digital imaging by Kristien Daem

p276-7 Collage © Johan Grimonprez

p278-9 Photography Theo Volpatti, © Theo Volpatti & Johan Grimonprez

p282-3 Photography Theo Volpatti, © Theo Volpatti & Johan Grimonprez

End papers Photography Theo Volpatti, © Theo Volpatti & Johan Grimonprez

Looking for Alfred
Johan Grimonprez

A Film and Video Umbrella/ Zapomatik co-production. In association with Centre for Fine Arts Brussels, The Photographers' Gallery and Anna Sanders Films. Made possible by the Flemish Audiovisual Fund and Arts Council England. Additional support from Deitch Projects, Riksutstillinger – The National Touring Exhibitions Norway, Yvon Lambert Gallery, Media Space Inc., Victoria and Productiehuis Rotterdam (Rotterdamse Schouwburg)

Head of Production
Bevis Bowden and Emmy Oost
Project Co-ordinator
Nina Ernst
Post-Production Paris
Corinne Castel
Cinematographer (DOP)
Martin Testar
Gaffer
Dirk Favere
Key Grip
Joris Vandezande
Sound Engineer
Raf Enckels
Art Director
Pol Heyvaert
Offline Editor
Nicolas Bacou
Sound Editor
Dominique Pauwels
Make-up
Diana Dreesen

Casting concept
Johan Grimonprez & Daragh Reeves

Tippi Hedren lookalike
Delfine Bafort

THE HITCHCOCK ACTORS

NEW YORK
David Stepkin, D. Michal Berkowitz, Peter Linari, Will Jordan, Matt Hyland, Gabor Morea, Jonathan Williams, Sean Ferguson, Leon Kurio, Leonard Tucker, Robert L. Haber, James Dickson, John Rainer, Ron Lee Savin, Don Amendolia, Jerome Nunziante, Kevin Carolan, Edgar Oliver, Sam Chan, Alan Kramer, Dominic Defilippis, Bruce Ho, Merwin Goldsmith, Robert Zanfini, Bo Kaprall
Casting by Caroline Sinclair

LOS ANGELES
Paul Hayes, Morris J. Seawright, Jules Fleming, Al Benner, Richard E. Coe, Zale Kessler, Barry Squitieri, Micki Schloss, Christopher Rocha, Thom Reed, Janice Davis, Alan Richards, Royce Herron, Steve Humphreys, David Alan Graf, Paul Morgan Fredrix, Robert Nino, Pete Leal, Vic Helford, Nicholas Worth, Howard George, Bob Rodriguez, Randall Bosley, Lyle Kanouse, Kathy Lamkin
Casting by Emily Schweber

LONDON
Frank Scantori, Robert Donald, Bill Moody, Peter Mairs, Glen Hayes, Ken Parry, David Adler, Peter Mairs, Richard Rycroft, Stephen Guy Daltry, Simon Fisher-Becker, Roger Swaine, Ron Burrage, Mark Perry
Casting by Chloe Emmerson

ROTTERDAM
Bob Bosma, A. van der Veer, A. van der Goes, Jan van de Boogerd, Jeffrey Cox, Jan Maas, Frans Noordt, Bas Bezemer
Casting by Pieter Leclerq, Productiehuis Rotterdamse Schouwburg

GENT
Ruud Gielen, José Bouchat, Ferdinant De Pièrre, Gerard Duquet, Freddy Verbust, Erik Grimonprez
Casting by Pol Heyvaert, Victoria

Johan Grimonprez would like to thank

Bernhart Schwenk, Reinhold Baumstark, Carla Schulz-Hoffmann (Pinakothek der Moderne); Steven Bode, Nina Ernst, Caroline Smith, Bevis Bowden (Film and Video Umbrella); Michael Van Peel, Emmy Oost (Zapomatik); Markus Hartmann (Hatje Cantz); Hartwig Garnerus (Theo Wormland Stiftung); Paul Dujardin, Sophie Lauwers, Elizabeth Vandeweghe, Dirk Snauwaert, Barbara Vanderlinden (Centre for Fine Arts, Brussels); Philippe Van Cauteren, Frank Maes (SMAK); Corinne Castel (Anna Sanders Films); Camilla Brown (The Photographers' Gallery, London); Flemish Audiovisual Fund; Arts Council England; Herman Lelie, Stefania Bonelli and Jessie; Annemie Vanackere (Productiehuis Rotterdamse Schouwburg); Dirk Pauwels; Marika Ingels (Victoria); Hisami Kuroiwa (Media Space Inc.); Jeffrey Deitch (Deitch Projects); Sean Kelly; Cecilia Casorati; Boshko Boskovic (Sean Kelly Gallery); Stale Stenslie (Riksutstillinger, National Touring Exhibitions, Norway); Maria Kodama; Steven Jacobs; Alain Kerzoncuf; Valerie Van Peel; Bart Vonck; Lieve and Patrick from Drukkerij Peeters; Liesbet Peeters; Yvon Lambert Gallery; Dieter Vermeulen; ACE Digital House; Labos Meuter-Titra; Nicolas Bacou; Peter Andersson; Olivier Bardet; Vanessa Bergonzoli; Stephane Pichard; Gert Everaart; Sophie Germain; Francine Grimonprez; Geraldine Grimonprez; Hollywood Hills House; Anne Mommens; Shirley Morales; Roberto Presciutti; Muriel Quancard; Michelle Kass Associates.

All the authors, actors, partners and photographers.

Jodie Bowler, 21, took the name of Mrs. Bowler-Hatt, when she married baker Chris Hatt, 27, of Frinton, Essex.

Daily Mirror June 24, 1995, 'Fortean Times Presents: Strange Days, The Year in Weirdness'

AUTHORS

Patricia Allmer is Research Associate at Manchester Metropolitan University's Manchester Institute for Research and Innovation in Art and Design (MIRIAD). She has published widely on René Magritte and Surrealism. She is the co-editor of the recently published book 'Collective Inventions: Surrealism in Belgium' and is the curator of the 2009 Manchester Art Gallery exhibition 'Angels of Anarchy: Women Artists and Surrealism'.

Jorge Luis Borges was born in Buenos Aires in 1899 but received most of his education in Europe. His collections of poems, essays, and short stories are among the most widely acclaimed writings of the 20th century. Borges was director of the Argentine National Library from 1955 until 1973. He died in Geneva in June 1986.

Chris Darke is a writer and film critic based in London. His work has appeared in 'Film Comment', 'Sight and Sound', 'Trafic', 'Cahiers du cinéma', 'Vertigo' and 'The Independent'. He is also the author of 'Light Readings: Film Criticism and Screen Arts', a monograph on Godard's *Alphaville* and 'Cannes: Inside the World's Premier Film Festival' (with Kieron Corless). He has directed occasional works including a video portrait of Chris Marker for the DVD of Marker's *La Jetée* and *Sans Soleil*.

Thomas Elsaesser is Professor in the Department of Media and Culture and Director of Research Film and Television at the University of Amsterdam. His essays on European cinema, film history and media archaeology, American cinema and contemporary media theory have been translated in more than 15 languages and published in over 200 collections. His most recent books as (co-) editor include: 'Cinema Futures: Cain, Abel or Cable?' (1998) and 'The Last Great American Picture Show' (2004). His books as author include 'Fassbinder's Germany: History, Identity, Subject' (1996), 'Weimar Cinema and After' (2000), 'European Cinema: Face to Face with Hollywood' (2005) and 'Terror und Trauma' (2007).

Tom McCarthy is a writer, artist and General Secretary of the International Necronautical Society. His first novel, 'Remainder' (Alma Books UK 2006/ Vintage US 2007), is currently being adapted for cinema by Film Four/Cowboy Films, and his second novel, 'Men in Space', is to be released in the UK in September 2007. He is also author of the non-fiction work 'Tintin and the Secret of Literature' (Granta Books 2006).

Jeff Noon is a British science fiction author. He has written several novels ('Vurt', 'Pollen', 'Automated Alice', 'Nymphomation', 'Needle in the Groove' and 'Falling out of Cars'), most of which are set in some version of his native city, Manchester. Other published works include a collection of short stories ('Pixel Juice'), newspaper and magazine articles, and a play ('Woundings').

Slavoj Žižek is a psychoanalyst and a dialectical-materialist philosopher. He is the current co-director of the International Centre for Humanities, at Birkbeck College, University of London. He is also the founder and president of the Society for Theoretical Psychoanalysis, Ljubljana. His latest publications include 'The Parallax View' (MIT Press, 2006) and 'How To Read Lacan' (Granta, 2007).

TEXTS

With thanks to Sidney Gottlieb for permission to use quotes from 'Hitchcock on Hitchcock: Selected Writings and Interviews', Ed. Sidney Gottlieb, University of California Press, Berkeley and Los Angeles, 1995.

'August 25, 1983', from 'Collected Fictions' by Jorge Luis Borges, translated by Andrew Hurley, copyright © 1998 by Maria Kodama; translation copyright © 1998 by Penguin Putnam Inc. Used by Permission of Viking Penguin, a division of Penguin Group (USA) Inc and Penguin Books Ltd.

'Hitchcock's women on Hitchcock: A panel discussion with Janet Leigh, Tippi Hedren; Karen Black; Suzanne Pleshette; and Eva Marie Saint': Gregg Garrett. Literature/Film Quarterly Vol. 21:2 (1999): 88.

The authors and publishers gratefully acknowledge the permission granted to reproduce the copyright material in this book.

Every effort has been made by the authors, contributors and editorial staff to trace holders of copyright and to obtain permission for the use of copyright material. The publishers apologise for any errors or omissions in this list. However, if any permissions have been inadvertently overlooked, please contact Zapomatik (at the address overleaf), so that any oversights can be corrected as soon as possible.

Looking for Alfred
Johan Grimonprez

Published by Film and Video Umbrella, Hatje Cantz Verlag, Pinakothek der Moderne and Zapomatik, with the support of Theo Wormland Stiftung, Arts Council England, The Flemish Authorities, Centre for Fine Arts, Brussels and SMAK Museum of Contemporary Art, Gent. With additional support from Sean Kelly Gallery and Deitch Projects.

Concept, castings and drawings by Johan Grimonprez

Edited by Steven Bode

Editorial assistance from: Nina Ernst (Film and Video Umbrella), Michael Van Peel and Emmy Oost (Zapomatik), Bernhart Schwenk (Pinakothek der Moderne)

Design by Herman Lelie and Stefania Bonelli

Printed in Italy by Amilcare Pizzi

© 2007 Film and Video Umbrella, Hatje Cantz Verlag, Pinakothek der Moderne, Zapomatik, the artist and the authors

Film and Video Umbrella
8 Vine Yard
London SE1 1QL
UK
Tel. +44 20 7407 7755
Fax +44 20 7407 7766
www.fvu.co.uk

Hatje Cantz Verlag
Zeppelinstrasse 32
73760 Ostfildern
Germany
Tel. +49 711 4405 200
Fax +49 711 4405 220
www.hatjecantz.com

Pinakothek der Moderne
Kunstareal München
Barer Strasse 40
D-80333 München
Germany
Tel. +49 8923 805 360
info@pinakothek.de
www.pinakothek.de

Zapomatik
Lange Steenstraat 16Q
B-9000 Gent
Belgium
info@zapomatik.com
www.zapomatik.com

Hatje Cantz books are available internationally at selected bookstores and from the following distribution partners:

USA/North America – D.A.P., Distributed Art Publishers, New York, www.artbook.com
Australia – Tower Books, Frenchs Forest (Sydney), www.towerbooks.com.au
France – Interart, Paris, www.interart.fr
Belgium – Exhibitions International, Leuven, www.exhibitionsinternational.be
Switzerland – Scheidegger, Affoltern am Albis, www.ava.ch

For Asia, Japan, South America, and Africa, as well as for general questions, please contact Hatje Cantz directly at sales@hatjecantz.de, or visit our homepage at www.hatjecantz.com for further information.

Distributed in Great Britain by Art Data
12 Bell Industrial Estate
5 Cunnington Street
London W4 5HB, UK
Tel. +44 20 8742 2319
www.artdata.co.uk

ISBN 978-3-7757-2008-3 (Hatje Cantz)
ISBN 978-1-904270-25-6 (Film and Video Umbrella)

Published in conjunction with the exhibition *Looking for Alfred*, Johan Grimonprez, at Pinakothek der Moderne, Munich May 10 – August 19, 2007

film and video umbrella

HATJE CANTZ

zapomatik

ARTS COUNCIL ENGLAND

with the support of the Flemish Authorities

S.M.A.K.
Stedelijk Museum voor Actuele Kunst. Gent

BOZAR EXPO

And somehow, the conversation led to his belly button. I don't know how. But he said, [as Hitchcock] 'You know, I don't have a belly button.' Well, I said, 'I think everyone has a belly button or they wouldn't have a mother.' And he said: 'No, I don't have a belly button.' And he literally sort of started undressing for me.
He pulled his shirt open, and in fact, Mr. Hitchcock did not have a belly button [laughter]. He'd had some kind of operation where they'd stitched it out [laughter].

Karen Black in 'Hitchcock's Women on Hitchcock: a panel discussion with Janet Leigh, Tippi Hedren, Karen Black, Suzanne Pleshette and Eva Marie Saint', 'Literature Film Quarterly', 1999 by Greg Garrett